JACK WELCH AND THE 4E'S OF LEADERSHIP

How to Put GE's
Leadership Formula to Work
in Your Organization

Jeffrey A. Krames

Author of the international bestseller
The Welch Way

McGraw-Hill

New York Chicago San Francisco Lisbon
London Madrid Mexico City Milan New Delhi
San Juan Seoul Singapore Sydney Toronto

2 3 4 5 6 7 8 9 0   DOC/DOC   0 1 0 9 8 7 6 5

ISBN 0-07-145780-1

First Edition

Jack Welch and The 4E's of Leadership is in no way authorized or endorsed by or affiliated with Jack Welch or General Electric. Nor is the book authorized or endorsed by or affiliated with Jeffrey Immelt, James McNerney, Larry Bossidy, Robert Nardelli, or Vivek Paul, or the companies they lead or were formerly associated with.

McGraw-Hill books are available at special quantity discounts to use as premiums and sales promotions, or for use in corporate training programs. For more information, please write to the Director of Special Sales, McGraw-Hill Professional, Two Penn Plaza, New York, NY 10121-2298. Or contact your local bookstore.

This book is printed on recycled, acid-free paper containing a minimum of 50% recycled, de-inked fiber.

Library of Congress Cataloging-in-Publication Data

Krames, Jeffrey A.
Jack Welch and the 4 E's of leadership : how to put GE's leadership formula to work in your organization / by Jeffrey A. Krames.— 1st ed.
    p.   cm.
Includes bibliographical references.
ISBN 0-07-145780-1 (hardcover : alk. paper)
    1. Leadership—Handbooks, manuals, etc.   2. Industrial management—Handbooks, manuals, etc.   I. Title.

HD57.7.K7255   2005
658.4'092—dc22   2005003985

To Nancy, Noah, and Joshua
My three miracles

CONTENTS

Contents

THE 4E LEADER: JACK WELCH'S WINNING LEADERSHIP FORMULA

The 4E Leader is the complete package.
He or she has great energy, can articulate a vision
and inspire others to perform, is a fierce competitor,
and consistently meets his or her financial goals.

The purpose of this book is fourfold:

1. *To explain clearly, and in depth, Jack Welch's 4E's Leadership model, known officially as the "four Es of GE Leadership": its history, development, and so on.* As you will learn, the 4E model evolved after Welch had been GE's chairman for more than a decade.

2. *To provide specific ways to apply the model that can be acted upon to enhance productivity throughout the organization.* Great ideas don't add value unless they are put to good use. Throughout the book, there are Best Practices of The 4E Leader that—if employed regularly—will make you and your organization more productive and successful.

3. *To validate the 4E model by calling upon other experts who can corroborate and elaborate upon elements of the model.* The work of leading thinkers is cited throughout the book, substantiating and building upon the original 4E Leadership model. Cited authors include such notables as Peter Drucker (*The Practice of Management*), Peter Senge (*The Fifth Discipline Fieldbook*), and Jim Collins (*Good to Great*).

4. *To show how the 4E model has impacted the "next generation" of great business leaders.* In Part 2 of the book, we will take an up-close look at how five "graduates" of the Welch leadership school applied what they had learned and what lessons can be gleaned from *their* actions and strategies.

While there have been dozens of books extolling the virtues of Jack Welch's business methods, little has been written about Jack Welch's 4E Leadership model. This is a glaring omission from the literature of management, because—as the record strongly argues—Jack Welch knows a great deal about what it takes to lead a large organization successfully, and the 4E Leadership model was central to that success.

In his 20-plus years at the helm of General Electric, Welch transformed a mature manufacturing company into an outstanding products-and-services juggernaut. He increased the value of the company more than 30 times over. He achieved all of this by defying some of GE's most venerated traditions (for example, by making hundreds of acquisitions), by making the "tough calls" (he laid off more than 100,000 workers), and by transforming GE's insular, hidebound culture (he fired the strategic planners and made sure that managers listened to workers).

But most of all, Welch selected and developed leaders. (During his tenure at the helm, GE turned out more Fortune 500 CEOs than any other company *in history*.) He once said, famously, that "the smartest people in the world hire the smartest people in the world," but the truth is that he looked for far more than smarts.

The discipline of the 4E's helped him to find and develop leaders who would fit into GE's high-octane, performance-based culture. Those who scored high on all four "E" categories were the ones who ultimately helped him fulfill his goal of building the world's most competitive organization.

What are the four characteristics shared by these exceptional leaders?

The 4E Leader has *energy*

The 4E Leader *energizes*

The 4E Leader has *edge*

The 4E Leader *executes*

Energy. Welch says that individuals with energy love to "go, go, go." We all know people like this—the ones with boundless energy, who get up every morning just itching to attack the job at hand. These are people who move at 95 miles per hour in a 55-mile-an-hour world.

Energizers know how to *spark others* to perform. They outline a vision and inspire people to act on that vision. Energizers know how to get people excited about a cause or crusade. They are selfless in giving others the credit when things go right and quick to accept responsibility when things go awry. Why? Because they know that sharing credit and owning blame *energizes* their colleagues.

3

Edge. Those with edge are *competitive* types. They know how to make the really difficult decisions, never allowing the degree of difficulty to stand in their way. These are leaders who don't hesitate to make what Peter Drucker calls the "life and death" decisions: hiring, promoting, and firing.

Execute. The first three E's are essential, but without *measurable results,* they are of little use to an organization. People who execute effectively understand that activity and productivity are not the same thing. The best leaders know how to convert energy and edge into action and results. They know how to execute.

The Linear E's

No one, including Jack Welch, argues that the 4E model is the be-all and end-all of leadership. For example, there are clearly prerequisites to the 4E's. Qualities like integrity, character, and work ethic are the "table stakes" of leadership—the price of admission. Absent these qualities, the leader will almost certainly prove deficient. A manager who is perceived as lacking in integrity, for example, may possess all the energy in the world. But he or she most likely won't have the respect of his or her colleagues or the moral compass with which to lead.

There are also qualities that "follow" the 4E's. During the last presidential primary season, Welch (in a *Wall Street Journal* op-ed piece) used the 4E model to evaluate the Democratic presidential contenders. (It should be noted that Welch is a self-professed Republican.) In rating the candidates, Welch included an additional component in his leadership formula: *passion.* Welch feels strongly that any leadership model must include passion. The best leaders are those who are filled with a fire-in-the-belly enthusiasm for what they do.

4

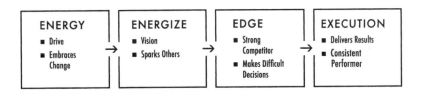

ENERGY	ENERGIZE	EDGE	EXECUTION
■ Drive ■ Embraces Change	■ Vision ■ Sparks Others	■ Strong Competitor ■ Makes Difficult Decisions	■ Delivers Results ■ Consistent Performer

Somewhere "in between" integrity and passion, therefore, are the 4E's. They overlap and interact, of course, and therefore they can't be lined up in a rigid sequence. Nevertheless, as depicted in the figure, there is a certain logical progression to them.

It all starts with energy. Without energy, a manager will have great difficulty energizing others. And a manager who is unable to energize others will lack edge and will have a hard time executing consistently.

Energizing is all about inspiring others, something that almost all leading management thinkers agree is a key to effective leadership. John Kotter of the Harvard Business School explains that leadership within a large and complex organization involves three "subprocesses."

In addition to establishing direction and aligning people, the leader has to have the ability to motivate and inspire—that is, to keep people "moving in the right direction despite major political, bureaucratic, and resource barriers to change by appealing to very basic, but often untapped, human needs, values, and emotions."

Jack Welch 101

There are few jobs as complex as that of the CEO of a large organization. Peter Drucker, the legendary management scholar, once wrote that the chief executive's job was every bit as complicated as directing an opera: "You have your stars and you can't give them orders; you have the supporting cast and the orchestra; you have the people behind the scenes; and you have your audience. Each group is completely different."

And hitting all the right notes is certainly much harder today than it was 50 years ago. In a recent 12-month stretch, 25 percent of the largest Fortune 500 companies' CEOs either quit or were fired.

Jack Welch became CEO of GE in 1981. That was, coincidentally, during a tumultuous period when many of the rules of the corporate game were dramatically and permanently altered. Globalization, the personal computer revolution, Michael Milken and his junk bonds, corporate restructuring—all these forces converged in the early 1980s to turn the business world upside down.

In his first years as CEO, as many observers inside and outside the company saw it, Welch did more to *ruin* General Electric than to rescue it. He believed that GE's size was severely hampering the company, which (as he saw it) had become slow and bureaucratic. When he took over, GE and its 43 "strategic business units" were held up as a model organization, but while GE was the talk of the business schools, its organizing principle had become a liability. Although GE's senior managers still had the swagger, the company's performance—and its stock price—was languishing.

You're either the best at what you do or you don't do it for very long.

In response to these perceptions, Welch acted decisively: selling off more than 100 businesses and firing more than 100,000 employees. After three years of gut-wrenching, DNA-level restructuring under Welch, few could recognize the proud old company.

But this was only the beginning. Welch called the massive restructuring just described the *hardware phase* of his transformation. The next phase (even more important to the company's well-being but even more fraught with peril) was what Welch called the *software phase*. This second transformational stage focused on boosting morale and productivity, two factors that Welch believed would either make or break GE in the decades to come.

To some extent, of course, Welch had brought the morale issue upon himself, through his dozens of divestitures and 100,000-plus layoffs. Now, he knew, he had to turn that around. He had to find a way to reach down into the depths of the company and effect major changes. He had to not only rebuild his employees' morale but also get them to perform at a *much higher* level. Getting back to zero wasn't enough; the company had to achieve unprecedented levels of productivity.

One key aspect of this challenge involved getting the company to switch from an internal perspective to an external, marketplace-oriented focus. He did this in part by replacing managers on a wholesale basis—swapping out internalists and swapping in individuals who were willing to take their cue from the marketplace. In time, he replaced almost all of the company's top managers, substituting his own handpicked "outside-in" choices.

But this was not a delegation of the responsibility for leading change—far from it! Throughout GE's far-reaching change process, Welch mainly led the charge himself. He took it as a given that people do not deal well with change. The only way his new ideas and strategies would take hold, he felt, would be if he

FOCUS ON THE OUTSIDE

The 4E Leader understands a critical lesson (taught by Peter Drucker and practiced by Jack Welch), which is that *results exist on the outside*, in the marketplace, where customers make decisions. Results do not live inside the halls of your company, no matter how hallowed those halls may be. "GE had been inside-out for more than a decade," Welch observed. "Outside-in is a powerful idea." He also promised that henceforth, his company would "never introduce a product . . . that hasn't been thought through from the customer's eyes."

directed the changes *himself,* personally. He would have to be the "front man" for all of his now-famous initiatives, ranging from his number 1, number 2 strategy to his Six Sigma initiative.

The story of how he achieved that—how he ultimately secured buy-in from hundreds of thousands of employees—contains essential lessons for managers in any size organization.

Evolution of The 4E Model

Jack Welch did not arrive at the vision of a 4E Leader all at once. In fact, he embraced several different leadership models along the way, each a refinement of the model that had preceded it.

In his first years as CEO, for example, Welch created a precursor to the 4E's. Its components were *head, heart,* and *guts.* "Head," of course, referred to an individual's intelligence and competence.

"Heart" connoted the "soft" skills of empathy and understanding, which Welch felt were essential to developing the open, candid organization that he was trying to build. "Guts," as the name implies, meant a level of self-confidence sufficient for making the tough decisions.

Welch believed that it was far easier to find leaders with "head" than it was to develop leaders with both "guts" and "heart." There are plenty of smart managers, as Welch saw it, but there aren't many who are both confident enough to make the tough calls and empathetic enough to foster candor and openness.

Welch's focus on the twin qualities of heart and guts may be surprising to some. After all, he earned a reputation for being a ruthless, "brainy" corporate leader. (In fact, he was named one of America's toughest bosses by *Fortune* magazine—a label he despised until the day he retired.)

However, from Welch's point of view, his own actions and the "head, heart, and guts" model were entirely consistent. As he saw it, firing nonperformers and selling off losing businesses *grew out of* his own embrace of head-heart-guts. He was a fiercely competitive leader who loved to win and who wanted his company to win. He had to come up with the right plan (head), make the tough decisions required by that plan (guts), and bring people along with him (heart).

WELCH'S FOUR TYPES OF LEADERS

The "head, heart, and guts" model carried Welch only so far. In the early 1990s, he put pencil to paper to describe what he called the four types of executives. This construct—very soon used to evaluate GE's managers—emerged as a potent tool in the Welch toolbox. Briefly described, those types were:

Type I leaders deliver on commitments (financial or otherwise) and share the values of the company. Obviously, these are the keepers.

Type II leaders miss financial goals and do not subscribe to the values of the organization. These leaders presented Welch with some of his easiest staffing decisions ("gone").

Type III leaders miss "short-term" commitments (i.e., revenue goals) but live the values of the company. These well-intentioned managers should be given another chance, said Welch (translation: they should be reassigned to a position that better suits their skills).

Type IV leaders deliver on commitments but don't share the values. This group presented Welch with some of his toughest decisions. What do you do with someone who consistently makes his or her numbers but flouts the company's value system?

This typology represented a new type of leadership assessment. Welch's signature appraisal—combining, as it did, strands of *performance* and *values*—became a model for other leaders to emulate.

Later Welch simplified the "four types" classification into a system of "A's," "B's," and "C's":

Type A's live the values and make the numbers. They articulate the vision of the company throughout the organization, while they take care of the company's business. These are the leaders whom Welch and his team worked hardest to retain.

Type B's live the values but do not always make the numbers. Again, Welch felt that these individuals should be given a chance to succeed—either in their current job or in another assignment.

Type C's do not live the values but may make the numbers. Ultimately, Welch concluded that managers (even highly productive ones) who did not live the organization's values should be terminated. In the long run, Welch argued, an organization can succeed only if the entire team is operating out of the same playbook.

Welch also concluded that in many cases, trying to convert a manager in the B or C category was more trouble than it was worth. "It is a wheel-spinning exercise," he explained. "Push C's onto B companies or C companies, and they'll do just fine …we are an A+ company. We want only 'A' players. We can get anyone we want. Take care of your best. Reward them. Promote them. Pay them well. Give them a lot of [stock] options."

THE 4E LEADER ELIMINATES THE CREDIBILITY GAP

Retaining people who do not live the values of your firm—who start turf wars, hog the limelight, or otherwise work against the firm's value system—ultimately creates a credibility gap. This is a trap that 4E Leaders stay out of. Because they understand the serious consequences of a double standard, they promote the A's and fire the C's. Keeping A's happy was a top Welch priority. Under him, GE kept 99 percent of its A players—and also did a thorough postmortem every time it lost one.

But there was more refining to be done. By the second half of the 1990s, Welch was developing yet another new leadership construct—one that would eventually lead him to the 4E's model.

THE FIVE-TRAITS DOCUMENT

One day in the summer of 1997, Welch sat down to compose a handwritten memo. (He still wasn't using computers much, back in those days.) He titled the memo "Best Leaders," and he began the memo by laying out what he took to be the traits of great managers.

At the top of the list were the qualities that would later evolve into three of the 4E's: *energy, energizes,* and *edge.* The five-traits document laid the foundation for Welch's 4E Leadership model, which he would articulate two years later.

In this document, Welch also argued strongly that the best leaders were the antithesis of "bureaucrats." Welch thought that "bureau-

THE 4E LEADER HATES BUREAUCRACY, DISPLAYS GREAT INTENSITY, AND SETS HIGH PERFORMANCE STANDARDS

The most effective leaders set a high performance standard for their direct reports and make sure that all are measured by that standard. They are candid with everyone, most especially those who do *not* perform. They understand that their credibility is on the line every day, and they strive to maintain and build on that credibility by promoting contributors and removing nonperformers.

crat" was one of the worst things you could call a leader. Bureaucrats play it safe; they don't embrace change, or "live speed" (a favorite Welchism), or come to work ready to rewrite their agendas. They muck up the works. Bureaucrats are the problem, not the solution. That's why Welch took every opportunity to rid the organization of momentum-killing bureaucracy.

Welch also associated the word *manager* with controlling and stifling individuals—a high-level sort of bureaucrat, but a bureaucrat all the same. That's why he made a point of calling his managers *leaders*.

WELCH'S WATERLOO?

Welch's record, as noted, was characterized by controversy throughout his many years as CEO and chairman of GE. Therefore, it came as little surprise to GE watchers that Welch's final, perhaps most daring move would turn out to be his most controversial.

In 2000, Welch attempted the boldest stroke of his career: the $45 billion acquisition of technology firm Honeywell. When Welch learned that the company was in play (United Technologies was about to make a tender offer for the company), he pounced by faxing a *handwritten* offer to the Honeywell board as it weighed the United Technologies offer. For months, it appeared as if Welch had snared the deal from the clutches of one of its rivals. However, when the deal disintegrated in 2001 (for antitrust reasons), critics were eager to declare Welch a failed actor, a leader who had lost his magic touch.

As a result of the acquisition that was not to be, the *Washington Post's* T. R. Reid, in his acclaimed book *The United States of Europe*,

(continued)

13

described Welch's final year as the obituary of his career. In a chapter entitled "Welch's Waterloo," Reid declares the following: "By ending his career with failure on a global scale, Welch had become a tainted figure, vulnerable now to criticism and second guessing from the fickle media and a business community that had previously put him on a pedestal."

Mr. Reid was right in at least one respect: The "fickle media" did indeed take their parting shots at Welch. That tradition has become a great American pastime: Make heroes and celebrities out of mere mortals, then knock them down later at the first sight of vulnerability.

Given all the incredible accolades Welch had garnered in recent years, this story was ripe for the picking. (Even the *Wall Street Journal* piled on by bringing in Welch's personal problems associated with his second failed marriage and an "excessive" retirement package. Welch later stanched this story by agreeing to rescind the retirement package and pay for what he had received thus far.)

However, despite all the pundits' predictions, Welch's "stock"—as measured in a variety of ways—suffered no knockout blow. When Welch released his leadership memoir, *Jack: Straight from the Gut*, on September 11, 2001 (the very same day of the terrorist attacks on the United States), buyers showed up in droves, helping Welch to sell close to a million copies of the lengthy book despite lukewarm reviews. This made *Jack* one of the most successful business books in history and helped justify the $7 million-plus advance Welch had received from Warner Books to pen the tome.

Thus, despite Welch's "transgressions," there was a substantial core Welch audience that was keenly interested in what he had to say.

Still, many U.S. managers believed that the Welch era had come to an end.

While many businesspeople in America may have seen Welch as somewhat tainted goods, the view from the East was far different. In Asia, Welch books topped best-seller lists long after the Honeywell acquisition had gone awry, right into 2003, 2004, and the first months of 2005. Asian readers seemed genuinely uninterested in the distractions that captivated U.S. business readers.

The book-buying behavior of businesspeople in those countries confirmed it: In places like Thailand, Singapore, Japan, and India, readers were far more interested in the *management methods* than in the man. They wanted to *be* Welch, or at least lead like him, and they cared little about the frivolous stories that consumed the Western media.

Businesspeople in those Asian countries understood something important about Welch that the "fickle" U.S. press corps did not. The fact that he was a CEO who had run into problems in his last year as CEO was besides the point; more pertinent was Welch's unmitigated success, and the fact that he had created a new business lexicon and methodology—a road map that showed managers a better way to run a large organization.

Put simply, they were more concerned with what Welch had done *right* than in what he had done *wrong*. And, as you will learn in Chapter 2, it is far more important to build on strength than to try to build on weakness. As Peter Drucker declared half a century earlier: "One can only build on strength . . . the greatest mistake is to try to build on weakness."

The GE Authentic Leadership Model

The E's were an abbreviated version of Welch's leadership ideal. The Authentic Leadership Model incorporated the 4E's but also described Welch's ideal leader in greater depth than any previous model or formula. This detailed model consisted of 12 traits that best describe the Welch leader, paraphrased as follows:

- *Strong leaders lead with character/integrity.* The best leaders are the most trustworthy.

- *Strong leaders have business competence/acumen.* They have an instinct for business—a "gut" that guides them well.

- *Strong leaders think global.* Welch's first companywide initiative was globalization, and he wanted all leaders to have a global mind-set.

- *Strong leaders are customercentric.* They understand Drucker's doctrine: Only a customer can define the purpose of a business.

- *They welcome change and disdain bureaucracy.* A manager once asked Welch what he should say when his people asked him when the changes would be over. Tell them the truth, Welch answered: "Change is never over."

- *Good leaders are strong communicators, and they are empathetic.* Authentic leaders not only know how to talk but also know how to listen. They are empathetic (have "heart") and do not bark out orders at subordinates.

- *Authentic leaders build effective teams.* The best leaders know that in order to meet or exceed their goals, they need the help of the best.

■ *The best leaders focus on achieving the objectives of the organization.* Individual contributions are meaningful only when they help the organization achieve its goals.

■ *The best leaders have great energy and spark others to perform.* The best leaders articulate a vision and get others to carry it out.

■ *Strong leaders have an "infectious enthusiasm."* This serves as a "force multiplier" as the organization's capabilities increase.

■ *Great leaders achieve and deliver.* They meet or exceed financial goals and other key objectives.

■ *The best leaders love what they do.* They get up each day ready to attack the job at hand. To them, work is not work; it's what they love.

The Authentic Leadership Model spelled out in detail the type of leader that Welch looked for. The best managers had a "boundaryless" style—Welch's signature term for an open, candid approach to leadership. As Welch used the term, boundaryless leaders are those who know that it is the *customer* who defines a business, who embrace change, hate bureaucracy, never ask anything of their employees that they would not do themselves, and are blessed with unlimited energy and potential.

They know how to *build a team* and how to *get results.* This is the brand of leader that helped Welch transform GE and turn it into the world's most valuable company.

Certainly one can see the roots of The 4E Leader in the Authentic Leadership Model. In some ways, the traits in this model are *implicit* in the 4E's. For example, "energizer" is most often someone who communicates well, has a good touch with customers, delivers results, and so on.

17

ARE YOU AN AUTHENTIC LEADER?

Some have said that Jack Welch was born to lead a large organization. For his part, Welch believed that leaders are *made*, not born. In the chapters that follow, each of the E's will be discussed at length, and at the end of each chapter, readers will have a chance to evaluate themselves and assess their own "E-quotient."

Before diving into the E's, take a few minutes to rate yourself on the 12 traits/characteristics in Welch's Authentic Leadership Model. In Welch's world, integrity and the ability to build trust are the cost of admission. But other qualities—the ability to think globally, build effective teams, spark others to perform— are the qualities that make all the difference after those initial thresholds have been reached.

Rate yourself against each of the traits on a 1-to-5 scale:

5 means that you strongly agree with the statement.

4 means that you agree with the statement.

3 means that the statement is not relevant to your work/ position.

2 means that you disagree with the statement.

1 means that you strongly disagree with the statement.

I have high integrity	1	2	3	4	5
I have great business instincts	1	2	3	4	5
I have a global perspective	1	2	3	4	5
I put customers first	1	2	3	4	5
I view change as an opportunity	1	2	3	4	5

I communicate effectively	1	2	3	4	5
I am a strong team builder	1	2	3	4	5
I help the organization to achieve its goals	1	2	3	4	5
I spark colleagues to perform	1	2	3	4	5
I have an infectious enthusiasm	1	2	3	4	5
I consistently meet or exceed financial goals	1	2	3	4	5
I love my work	1	2	3	4	5

Now add up your score. If your tally is:

50 or above: You have the right stuff (at least by your own estimation)! Welch would call you an "A player."

40–49: You are on solid footing, and you have the raw materials to be an authentic leader.

30–39: You have room for improvement. But take heart: By acting on the action and to-do items that follow, you can enhance your leadership skills and development.

20–29: This is a below-average score. You lack either experience or natural leadership ability. To aid in your development, consider getting a mentor. Also, enroll in leadership courses, voraciously read everything you can get your hands on, and *keep at it.* Persistence is another key leadership quality.

<20: By your own assessment, you are in Welch's bottom 10 percent. Not everyone is cut out to lead. One reason is this: While many aspects of leadership can be learned, qualities like character, integrity, and trustworthiness cannot be taught (at least not to an adult).

The 4E Leader To-Do List

☐ **Develop an outside-in perspective.** To ensure that you are getting an outside-in perspective of your firm and its offerings, visit the same "showrooms" as your customers. Go out into your market(s), wherever they may be. By consistently living in your customer's shoes, you will have a chance to see your business through your customer's eyes—a hugely important advantage in today's fast-moving marketplace.

☐ **Wage a war on bureaucracy.** Make this a priority! (Welch targeted GE's bureaucracy from the very start.) Eliminate needless forms and approvals. Create cross-functional teams to eliminate silos. Help knock down walls by encouraging anyone in the company to send you an e-mail, regardless of rank and location. Symbolic? No—real! Part of eliminating bureaucracy is eliminating the boundaries that separate senior managers from the employees who perform the lion's share of the work.

☐ **Hire and promote passionate leaders.** Passion can't be faked. Look to hire and promote energetic people who are passionate about what they do. That will pay great dividends down the line.

☐ **Find new ways to make the organization more customercentric.** This was an important piece of the Welch Authentic Leadership Model. The 4E Leader understands that it is the customer who determines "value" and who holds the key to the future of your business. Spend more time with customers, and insist that your colleagues do the same.

☐ **Make sure that employees who live by the values of the organization are given a chance to succeed—at least up to the point of diminishing returns.** Employees who have character and integrity and who live by the code of the company may be a foundation upon which you can build part of your future. But don't beat your head on the wall trying to convert the unconvertible.

☐ **Use Welch's 12 authentic leadership points when reviewing your top people and evaluating new hires.** During your next set of performance reviews, rate your people against the 12 points of the Authentic Leadership Model. Write the points down on a sheet of paper, and rate your subordinates on those characteristics. This can be used as a differentiation tool to grade employees (see more on differentiation in Chapter 3).

PART 1

THE 4E'S OF
LEADERSHIP

Part 1 of the book devotes a chapter to each of The 4E's of Leadership. Peter Drucker once declared the primary— and most complex task of a manager—is to "manage managers," and he later elaborated on this by defining *managers* more broadly to encompass all "knowledge workers" (anyone who performs a job for which some formal education is required).

The chief goal (and chief challenge, I might add) of compiling the following four chapters was to showcase each of the E's while simultaneously "connecting the dots" by showing, in systematic fashion, just what it takes to effectively "manage managers" while creating a performance-based learning organization.

Connecting the dots, then, in proper sequence emerged as one of the key priorities of Part 1. That's because there is a logical *progression* of tasks and initiatives that must be achieved in order to manage and/or transform any organization.

Let's take Chapter 1, the "energy" chapter, as an example. In it, the concept of energy is examined from a variety of perspectives. There is physical energy, of course, but in a social institution such as a corporation, there is a level of energy that transcends the individual. A firm's organizational energy is determined by many factors, including its structure, processes, culture, norms of behavior, and so on.

Welch spent years in an ardent crusade to rid the firm of anything that interfered with energy and productivity while adding initiatives that would spark energy and enhance performance. The simple flowchart below takes several title sections from the first chapter to show the progression of Welch's leadership makeover of GE:

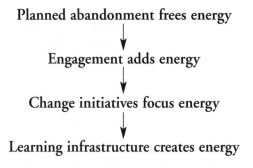

Planned abandonment frees energy

↓

Engagement adds energy

↓

Change initiatives focus energy

↓

Learning infrastructure creates energy

Welch was successful not because he had some magic formula or overnight quick fix, but because he made the right calls. He did decisive things that "moved the needle" and implemented them in a sequence that greatly increased his chances for success. Part 1 of this book is intended to shine the light on these initiatives while bringing in the "voices" of other management thinkers to provide specific recommendations on creating a results-based organizational culture.

CHAPTER 1

THE 4E LEADER
HAS *ENERGY*

*Welch's ideal leaders have boundless reserves of energy
and a strong penchant for action. They embrace
change and love the thrill of the game.*

It all begins with energy. Leaders must have other strengths,
such as intelligence and decision-making ability, but it is
energy that converts good ideas into measurable performance.

Strictly defined, *energy* means a source of power, whether elec-
trical, mechanical, or otherwise. But for our purposes, there is
more to energy than its physical properties. In addition to physical energy, there is also mental energy and what might be called
"emotional energy"—the kind of energy that a leader projects to
help build the spirit or morale of an organization.

It is an energy that reaches across people and binds together individual contributions into a purposeful whole. In that sense, emotional energy can be as important as or *more* important than
physical energy. Emotional energy is the passion that gets the job
done.

Passion, not Charisma

Some books on leadership point to something called "charisma" as an essential quality of a great leader. But when Jack Welch talks about the importance of passion as a component of effective leadership, he is talking about something very different from charisma. In fact, charisma (which we'll define here as the quality of personal magnetism) has little to do with effective leadership. Peter Drucker has made this point in many of his works.

John F. Kennedy was one of the most charismatic presidents in recent history, Drucker points out, but he failed to *accomplish* very much. Conversely, Drucker has also written that Dwight D. Eisenhower and Harry Truman had the charisma of "dead mackerel" but were extremely effective leaders.

Having passion, says Welch, "doesn't mean loud or flamboyant. It is something that comes from deep inside." But although the wellsprings of passion are internal, the workplace in which one finds oneself can be either supportive or destructive of passion. The best organizations, Welch argues, spark and nurture a person's passion.

What kind of company nurtures passion? A company that encourages frank dialogue and candid communications and—conversely—rejects autocratic behavior, turf wars, and other behaviors that impede effective communications.

Passion is a *fuel.* As such, it can be put to the wrong purposes. Lacking good guidance, people can become passionate about the wrong things. For example, they may come to crave the limelight, put their personal goals above the goals of the organization, build fiefdoms, and so on. But again, these behaviors are destructive because they work against an open, candid organization.

THE 4E LEADER HIRES FOR PASSION

Passion cannot be taught or learned. The best way to build a passionate team is to hire people who share your excitement for the job at hand. When interviewing candidates, ask them questions that help you to determine their values, priorities, and so on. You're looking for that rare mix: people who want to feel passionate about their jobs but are also willing to subjugate their personal goals and rewards for the good of the organization.

Simplify the Organization

Getting high-energy people into the company is only the first step—the organizational equivalent of setting the table. The next, and bigger, task is to create an organization that *converts energy into results.* Early in his tenure at GE, Welch set his sights on simplifying the organizational chart. Why? Because when he surveyed GE's structure in the early 1980s, he saw a complex, lumbering, muddled organization with too many management layers, too many titles, too much of everything. To his eyes, the structure made no sense: 25,000 managers, more than 130 vice presidents, and more strategic planners than any one company would ever need.

With a speed and determination that shocked many of his colleagues, Welch delayered the company. He fired the strategic planners and put the responsibility for plotting the direction of each of the business units back into the hands of the people who led those units.

Later, he launched his now-legendary Work-Out™ initiative, aimed at getting good ideas out of the entire workforce (and, of course, compelling management to *deal* with those ideas). In all cases, Welch had three key goals in mind: making the organization more productive, weaving higher levels of self-confidence into the fabric of the firm, and throttling bureaucracy.

We have already introduced the subject of bureaucracy, which we revisit here because Welch saw it as an enormous energy drain on the organization. Bureaucracy kills passion and (as Peter Drucker notes) diverts energy from the critical tasks at hand: "The higher up an executive, the larger will be the proportion of time that is not under his control and yet not spent on contribution. The larger the organization, the more time will be needed just to keep the organization together and running, rather than make it function or produce."

Drucker has identified one of the great management traps. In many companies, senior managers find most of their time consumed by simply keeping the trains running on time. Of course, the opposite *should* be true: The higher one climbs on the ladder of a complex organization, the more time one should have available to come up with new ways of looking at things. But in a highly bureaucratic organization, senior managers spend much of their time putting out fires or simply trying to get the organization to move off the dime. Passion and productively suffer accordingly.

Welch, an enthusiastic student of Drucker, recognized this intuitively. He was relentless in his determination to make GE the world's most productive organization, focusing on key metrics of productivity such as inventory turns. The first two steps in this direction, as noted, were a wholesale destruction of the bureaucracy

THE 4E LEADER CUTS
THROUGH COMPLEXITY

Too many layers and too much bureaucracy can stifle productivity and muck up the works. The 4E Leader understands that the organization should be designed to harness—and amplify—the collective energy of the organization so that the whole is more than the sum of its parts.

and a simplification of the organizational structure. But these steps alone, Welch knew, would not be enough. In addition, he had to make sure that employees and managers were exposed to new ideas—and given ample opportunity to soak up those new ideas.

Therefore, even while he was making drastic budget cuts elsewhere, he invested heavily in Crotonville, GE's management training institute on the Hudson River, north of New York City.

Crotonville became the de facto headquarters of Welch's organizational transformation—a place where GE's best and brightest could go to both expand their intellectual horizons and recharge their batteries. *Fortune* called Crotonville "Harvard on the Hudson."

Welch considered Crotonville to be the glue that held the company together through all the change initiatives. Crotonville, he said, served as a "forum for the sharing of the experiences, the aspirations, and, often the frustrations of the tens of thousands of GE leaders who passed through its campus."

Welch, obviously, was one of those leaders himself. He loved to mix it up with managers at Crotonville (a source of energy for him), and he also picked up valuable ideas in the Crotonville sessions. In fact, he credits one management class that he attended with contributing significantly to refining his signature "number 1, number 2 strategy."

There were many other senior executives who benefited from the Crotonville experience. One such executive, Robert Nardelli (former CEO of GE Aircraft Engines and CEO of Home Depot), reflected on this in early 2005: "...I was afforded a tremendous amount of opportunities at GE to learn a variety of different businesses and a variety of different markets. And the company made a tremendous investment in me and other leaders in Crotonville through educational programs and leadership forums."

Planned Abandonment Frees Energy

One way to ensure that the energy of an organization is not drained or inappropriately diverted is to *abandon* things—specifically, those tasks, processes, and products that no longer add value to the firm. Peter Drucker popularized the concept of "planned abandonment," which, like simplification, can play a vital role in freeing energy and raising productivity.

Welch learned about planned abandonment from Drucker himself. The week before Welch took over as CEO of GE, he met with Drucker at the latter's home in Claremont, California. At that meeting, the two men—the management guru and the incoming CEO—discussed Welch's opening moves as GE's chief executive.

Drucker made the case that the company had been in a period of retrenchment for most of the 1970s. The time had come, he said, for the company to go on the offensive. Drucker and Welch agreed that GE needed to shed those businesses that could not live up to one of Drucker's most fundamental business litmus tests:

> *If you were not already in a business, would*
> *you enter it today, knowing what you know?*

Welch decided that in many cases GE's answer had to be no. Then he *acted* on those decisions. He sold off GE's small-appliance division, and three years later he traded away the company's consumer electronics business (which it had gained in the RCA acquisition). He divested them because neither of them passed the Drucker litmus test.

As it turned out, exiting these businesses was essential to GE's future because it freed up both energy and resources, allowing the company to focus on its strengths: (1) high-technology businesses, such as aircraft engines and medical products, (2) core businesses, such as lighting, and (3) service businesses like GE Capital.

THE 4E LEADER JETTISONS PRODUCTS AND/OR BUSINESSES THAT DO NOT FIT THE VISION

In order to properly allocate resources and maximize productivity, The 4E Leader jettisons products or divisions that are not strategic—that is, any business that cannot be grown or does not fit the vision. Businesses in which the firm has (or can soon create) some sort of competitive advantage should be the main concern of top management.

Energy and Change

Of all the words and ideas in the Welch lexicon, few are as important as *change*. Welch knew that everything was changing—the marketplace, GE's customers, the competitive landscape, and so on—and that he had to get ahead of that change.

From the moment he assumed leadership, therefore, his words and actions combined to send an unmistakable message: *The status quo is not good enough.* Single-digit growth is not good enough; the tried and true is not good enough; business as usual is not good enough; yesterday is not good enough.

At the same time, he had to get his people to see change not as a threat but as an opportunity. That new mind-set would help to grow and channel the energies of the organization, thereby boosting productivity and effectiveness.

None of this would happen overnight, of course. Most leaders underestimate how long it takes to bring about genuine culture change. Welch was no exception; he was constantly chiding himself for not moving fast enough. He learned that even though he was aiming for *speed*—for large changes as quickly as possible—he would achieve true success only over the long haul.

Ultimately, he prevailed. His focus on change as an opportunity rather than a threat ultimately created the kind of energy that he had hoped to foster. Despite the disruptions that Welch had imposed on the organization, GE's employees now understood that *change was good.* The perception of change had been altered and was now a source of organizational energy. Writing in his last year as CEO, Welch observed (with obvious pride) that change was now "in the genes" of every employee: "We breathe it in our blood every day, now is the time to change the game."

How can a leader add energy to the organization during any large-scale change effort? The 4E Leader follows these important steps:

THE SEVEN STEPS OF DEALING WITH CHANGE

1. *Explain the new rules of engagement.* Go to great lengths to explain exactly what you are trying to achieve. In his first speeches as CEO, Welch explained that his goal was to create a company in which all the businesses were tops in their markets. That signaled to employees, loudly and clearly, that he would keep only businesses that were market leaders.

2. *Deal with change head-on.* Welch tackled change by owning it, spotlighting it, and incorporating it into the company's shared values. "Change is continual, thus nothing is sacred. Change is accepted as the rule rather than the exception." Change was a constant theme at Welch's company. Legendary football coach Vince Lombardi once said that "winning is not a sometime thing." Welch felt precisely the same way about change—and, not incidentally, about winning.

3. *Paint a vivid picture of the finish line.* Get employees and managers to share a vision of the future. Explain clearly the metrics that will be used to measure success so that people steer toward success and recognize it when they see it. Why did Welch's company enjoy double-digit growth, faster inventory turns, and so on? One of the essential success factors was Welch's ability to get all its leaders and employees to read from the same (explicit) sheet of music.

4. *Candor first, foremost, and always.* Candor, openness, trust, boundarylessness: These were the watchwords that described Welch's ideal organization. He knew from

unhappy personal experience that organizations that lacked these characteristics were energy-drainers. He believed that the opposite was true as well. He also knew that people took their cues from the top, and he made sure that he practiced what he preached.

5. *Overcommunicate.* In the same spirit, Welch served personally as the "champion" of all his strategies and initiatives. When implementing a key initiative, such as globalization or Six Sigma, he repeated the particular mantra at hand so frequently that (as he later recalled) he nearly gagged on his own words. But it was a small price to pay, he felt, for the kind of clarity that leads to energy and productivity.

6. *Exploit the opportunities that change brings.* Change is often a positive thing. Under Welch, GE made more than 1,200 acquisitions—an absolutely astounding number. That change gave all GE's business leaders a chance to grow their businesses by means of acquisitions, and it fueled the majority of GE's growth during the Welch years.

7. *Reiterate that change never ends.* When do change, turmoil, disruption, and upset end? Never, said Welch: *We've just begun.* The trick is not to make change go away; the trick is to change the way you think about it. The force of change can increase many times over when certain key variables are changed. One executive who grasped this reality is Robert Nardelli. In his first months as Home Depot CEO he was sharply criticized for his early moves. Some thought that Nardelli was the wrong man to lead the retailing giant. After all, he had no experience in retail.

He understood that change fills people with fear, both inside and outside of the company:

> *Any time there is a change whether it was the change*
> *that took place at GE, whether it was the change*
> *that took place at Honeywell with Larry [Bossidy] or*
> *certainly in my case, probably the anxiety level was*
> *higher because it was such a dramatic change from*
> *one industry to another, from heavy industrial to*
> *another…part of the angst was the result of the*
> *speed with which the change took place.*

Once again, the key is how a leader deals with change that often determines the difference between success and failure. Those leaders that welcome change—and instill that quality in their direct reports and colleagues—are the ones that win the most consistently.

Engagement Adds Energy

Welch also learned that to truly inspire and engage, you had to give people a platform to contribute new ideas. Jim Collins, author of the best-selling business book *Good to Great*, learned this after he and his 20-member research team conducted more than 15,000 hours of research into the ingredients that make up a great company: "A primary task in taking a company from good to great is to create a culture wherein people have a tremendous opportunity to be heard and, ultimately, for the truth to be heard."

More than a decade before those words were written, Welch created Work-Out, the breakthrough initiative that forever changed the culture of GE. Work-Out is the town hall–style meeting that Welch created to give employees a forum for speaking out. In a

FLYING HIGH ON ENERGY AND PASSION

One business leader who consistently showed his energy and passion was Southwest Airlines' feisty founder, Herb Kelleher. In a period when most of his larger rivals were racking up multibillion-dollar losses, Kelleher was delivering steady growth and profits, year after year, and winning industrywide customer service awards. What was his secret?

Like Welch, Kelleher reinvented the management rulebook. Among other things, he *hired for passion*, thereby creating a unique service organization that was known for its positive attitude and good humor. "If you are not on fire about what you're doing, why you're doing it, and the people who do it with you," he explained, "then you can't kindle their minds, hearts and devotion to a cause."

In addition to hiring for passion, he argued that the organization should let people be themselves at work—and then go even farther. The company, he wrote, should "celebrate the achievements of [its] people, often and spontaneously."

Southwest became legendary for celebrating the milestones experienced by its employees, including their weddings, births, marriages, and other happy moments—and also for acknowledging and sharing in employees' losses and catastrophes, which is almost unheard of in large corporations.

The point? Kelleher's actions added energy to the organization. He valued informal dialogue. He urged his managers to speak from the heart, as well as from the head. He underscored the idea that *job titles* aren't important but that *leadership qualities* are. Kelleher believed strongly that an organization's two most important constituencies are its employees and its customers—in that order. "Employees are your premier customers," argued Kelleher. If the company succeeds in involving and inspiring its employees, they become more tolerant and more empathetic—toward each other and also toward their external constituencies.

Source: Jeffrey Krames: *What the Best CEOs Know*,
pp. 189–191.

typical Work-Out session (which Welch made a voluntary program at first so that people could ease into it), there are two keys to making it work:

1. Participants must be bold enough to tell their bosses—nose to nose—exactly what needs to be done in order to make the business better.

2. Bosses must be able to say yes or no right then and there (or, in rare instances, "I will get back to you within a specified period of time when I have more information").

Work-Out turned the hierarchy upside down. Why? Because in a Work-Out session, it is the people who are lower on the chain of command who get to tell the bosses how to do things better. Before that, few GE workers were given any real platform to express themselves. That was why Work-Out was such a seminal program and why it effectively paved the way for much that would come later.

Welch also understood that energy did not stop with the individual. It is incumbent upon the organization to foster and harness individual energy in order to achieve organizational objectives. What good is the energetic individual if he or she is frustrated at every turn by the organization's bureaucracy and red tape?

Welch recognized this early on, and through a variety of methods, he took aim at GE's labyrinth of bureaucracy. His ultimate goal was an organization that was free of bureaucracy—one in which ideas flowed freely. Later, he would characterize his leadership ideal as the "boundaryless" organization.

Boundarylessness—the somewhat awkward word that Welch made up to describe an open, candid organization that was free of bureaucracy and turf wars—became the management concept most closely associated with the former GE chairman. Information flows freely throughout a boundaryless enterprise; anything that gets in the way of candor, the flow of ideas, and the conduct of productive meetings simply *must* be dealt with.

Other management thinkers agreed with Welch and subscribed to the principles behind his Work-Out initiative and the concept of boundarylessness. Again, from Jim Collins: "Leading from good to great means having the humility to grasp the fact that you do not yet understand enough to have the answers and then to ask the questions that will lead to the best possible insights." Although Collins was not writing specifically about Work-Out, his summary certainly captures the spirit of Work-Out.

Collins also subscribed to Welch's "face reality" edict, which could correctly be called Welch's first law of business. Collins put it this way: "Leadership is about creating a climate where the truth is heard and the brutal facts confronted."

Absent candor and "the brutal facts," boundarylessness is simply not possible.

THE 4E LEADER STRIVES FOR BOUNDARYLESSNESS

Anything that builds walls—between departments, between the company and the customer—must be destroyed. Bureaucracy must go. Noise in the system must be throttled back. This is an iterative process that takes months and years, not days or weeks. Implementing Work-Out or other similar confidence-building sessions can help, but these actions must be part of a larger effort to rid the company of debilitating energy diverters.

Change Initiatives Focus Energy

Given the sheer enormity of GE (with more than 300,000 employees) and the vast number of businesses under the corporate umbrella, Welch could have wound up with a company in which people went off in all directions, "doing their own things." To make sure that did not happen—and to make sure that everyone was reading from the same sheet of music—Welch strengthened what he called the company's "operating system."

This somewhat bland phrase actually comprised the specific processes whereby the company drove knowledge and intellect sharing throughout the company. As Welch explained, "It is a year-round series of intense learning sessions where business CEOs, role models, and initiative champions meet and share intellectual capital."

GE spread its knowledge largely through two key vehicles: through its regular meetings and reviews, and through the more sweeping companywide initiatives such as Work-Out and Six Sigma.

The regularly scheduled meetings included Welch's yearly senior managers' meeting in Boca Raton, Florida. It was at this event, which included 600 of GE's top managers, that Welch usually unveiled one of his major company crusades, like Six Sigma. Other regularly scheduled meetings included Session C (in which all senior GE managers were appraised) and the management classes at Crotonville. All the meetings also served to maintain momentum for one or more of the companywide initiatives.

At the heart of GE's operating system were the company's shared values. Being open to new ideas, disdaining bureaucracy, being customer-driven, striving for simplicity and boundarylessness—all of these helped to define the company and its people. Another stated goal of the operating system was to "channel and focus the torrent of ideas and information" generated by GE's managers and employees.

Welch's major change initiatives played a key role in making the company more focused and more competitive. Under his leadership, GE launched five major initiatives, including programs like Work-Out, Six Sigma, and Digitization. These were complex, intricate programs, usually involving hundreds of thousands of employees. In implementing Six Sigma, for example, thousands of GE managers switched jobs, taking on new roles as "black belts" and "master black belts" and volunteering to undergo hundreds of hours of new training.

Welch also saw the potential for a "virtuous circle." Meetings, performance reviews, annual events: All were intended to improve corporate performance by enhancing the contributions of managers and employees. Logically speaking, Welch reasoned, if he could improve the quality of these meetings, reviews, and performance appraisals, then performance might well follow.

And it should be stressed that GE didn't hold meetings or training in fits and starts. In fact, the company called meetings and conducted reviews on a year-round basis.

Susan Frank, a contributor to *The Fifth Discipline Fieldbook*, wrote of the importance of having frequent meetings to talk about the "vision" and "reality" of the organization. "It seems so simple at first glance . . . but personal mastery takes a lot of practice. Only 10 to 15 percent of all participants who attend training programs can consistently apply the insights and skills they learned back in the workplace. Typically, they simply run out of steam. Under stressful situations, they can't generate the energy to master and apply new skills, so they revert back to old habitual ways of doing things."

Learning Infrastructure Creates Energy

Of course, Welch's operating system and initiatives were not ends unto themselves but rather means to an end. Welch's ultimate goal was to create a learning culture inside the halls of GE. Peter

THE 4E LEADER STRENGTHENS THE OPERATING SYSTEM

Senior managers must build an operating system that is tailored to help achieve the aims of the organization. The 4E Leader knows that every employee meeting, whether planned or not, is an opportunity to reinforce important parts of the company "story." It is vital that this story be passed on in meetings, in training, and in performance reviews.

Senge, the lead author of *The Fifth Discipline Fieldbook* and a pioneer in organizational learning, explains that leaders who are seeking to develop a learning organization must concentrate on three "architectural design elements." Without all three, asserted Senge, the attempt to develop a learning organization will fail.

1. *"Without guiding ideas, there is no passion, no overarching sense of direction or purpose."* Welch used shared values, meetings (formal and informal), training at Crotonville, and company wide initiatives to provide a sense of purpose. He seldom missed an opportunity to hammer away at the importance of initiatives like Six Sigma or digitization. As a result, people were not wandering the halls questioning the motives and practices of management.

   Welch was hard-nosed on these core points. In fact, he went far farther than any other large-company CEO in the direction of "putting people to the sword." He told them bluntly that if they could not live by the company's values, they should find work elsewhere. At first, even his senior managers balked at what they regarded as a draconian policy. But Welch persisted and prevailed: *Put up or get out.* People soon learned that his edicts had teeth.

2. *"Without theory, methods, and tools,"* explains Senge, *"people cannot develop the new skills and capabilities required for deeper learning."* Most employees see change initiatives as fleeting—a banner-waving fad that must be endured. This is why most change efforts fail. Welch understood this intuitively, and as a result, he embraced major initiatives carefully and cautiously. This is why, for example, he was not sold on Six Sigma from the start. He thought it was just another fad. Once he was convinced that it was a genuine, quantitative, and measurable way

to boost quality and lower costs, he launched the program with full force, becoming a self-proclaimed Six Sigma "fanatic."

Welch's approach to Six Sigma serves as an excellent example of how to launch a successful change initiative. First, and most important, it was a *bottom-up* initiative. It all started with the employees. In 1995, employees told Welch (in the company's annual survey) that the quality of GE's products was not cutting it. He then launched the program at his annual managers' meeting, before rolling it out to the rest of the company. GE made sure that both theory and tools were available in abundance.

The key is to make sure that your organization provides employees with both the platform and the means to assist them in their learning. It is not enough to "engage" employees once a year or to preach learning on the company intranet.

People need to understand that learning and intellect sharing are company priorities and that all of management is committed to them. The only real way to do this is to provide employees with a wide variety of ways to learn, thus embedding education and knowledge sharing deep into the fabric of the company.

3. *"Without innovations in infrastructure,"* wrote Senge, *"inspiring ideas and powerful tools lack credibility because people have neither the opportunity nor the resources to pursue their visions or apply the tools."* Although he is using different words, Senge is clearly referring to the operating system. Welch took many important steps to make sure that the company's infrastructure (its operating system) provided a solid foundation on which he could anchor his change initiatives.

Before he took over as CEO, for example, GE's senior managers held the corporate learning facility at Crotonville in generally low esteem. Attendance at a Crotonville program was seen as a booby prize—or, worse, a punishment and humiliation for managers whose careers had stalled.

The *stars* certainly did not go there. Welch himself had attended only *one* management-training course in the years before becoming CEO. He was determined to change all of that by innovating and investing in infrastructure.

Accordingly, Welch invested heavily in Crotonville. He worked with consultants to develop the company's shared values. He also made sure that there was an intricate system of meetings in place, such as the CEC meeting (the most senior managers' meeting, which took place every 90 days) and annual management reviews (Session C).

Through his words and deeds, Welch put a premium on learning and new ideas. He stated unequivocally that at *his* GE, it was

THE THREE ARCHITECTURAL DESIGN ELEMENTS OF ORGANIZATIONS

1. Guiding ideas

2. Theories, methods, and tools

3. Innovations in infrastructure

Source: Senge, *The Fifth Discipline Fieldbook*, p. 37.

the quality of the idea that mattered most—not the number of "stripes on one's shoulder."

Senge concluded that the number of companies that actually embraced all three of these guiding ideas was, in fact, surprisingly small. Companies were missing out on a golden opportunity because (as Senge also asserted) when all three of these ideas are put in place, then further innovations in infrastructure occur far more easily and are more easily sustained. People are also more likely to take risks without the approval of management.

This last point was a vital one for Welch. From day one, he sought to remove what he called the "shackles from the feet" of his employees.

ASSESS YOUR "ENERGY" QUOTIENT

How much energy do you have? Remember that energy is about far more than the physical. There is mental energy, agility (the ability to make adjustments in strategy and goals as the situation dictates), as well as emotional energy. Some organizations are designed to harness the energy of their best performers, while others thwart their employees at every turn. Answer the following questions to see how you—and your organization—stack up:

1. Do you wake up each morning ready to attack the job at hand?

2. Do you view change as more of an opportunity than a threat?

3. When implementing any large-scale change effort, do you paint a vivid picture of the finish line?

(continued)

---

4. Do you hire for attitude and passion?

5. Do you look to cut through complexity and formality?

6. Do you practice "planned abandonment" by cutting unprofitable product lines and/or divisions?

7. Do you give people a platform to express their opinions and come up with new ideas (e.g., akin to Welch's Work-Out sessions)?

8. When people do come up with new ideas, is there a system in place to act on them in a timely manner (i.e., an operating system)?

9. Do you engage your direct reports in meaningful dialogue and provide constructive feedback on a consistent basis?

10. Are people in your organization encouraged to take calculated risks (i.e., not punished when those risks don't pan out)?

Take a moment to tally up the "yes" answers, giving yourself a point for each one. If you scored:

8 or above: Chances are that you are a leader who is rich in energy. Go on to the "energize" chapter secure in the knowledge that you, and your organization, are well positioned for growth and success.

6–7: Not a bad score, but there is room for some fine-tuning.

5 or fewer: If you scored 5 or fewer, you—and your organization—may be in dire need of an overhaul. The next chapters will help you to figure out the specific areas that require the greatest amount of reengineering. After reading the to-do items at the end of this chapter, go on to the next chapters, and be sure to complete the assessment exercises that appear at the end of each chapter.

The 4E Leader To-Do List

☐ **Review all forms and approvals generated by your department, and seek to eliminate three of the most archaic.** Every business has forms and approvals that make little sense, but that have persisted because no one has bothered to rethink them.

☐ **Make training a top priority—inside and outside the classroom.** Much of the best "training" inside a company happens informally, outside the classroom, in informal meetings, discussions, reviews, and so on. The 4E Leader understands that every interaction offers an opportunity for learning and seeks to maximize informal meetings and dialogue.

☐ **Conduct an audit of all departmental meetings and reviews, and jettison those that add no value.** Then take the time to figure out what is needed by making a list of the specific behaviors and skills that are needed to do the job at hand. Generate a list of meetings and training topics that, if added to your company's repertoire, would be likely to lead to improved performance.

☐ **Follow the Welch rules on dealing with change.** Welch dealt with change head-on, fostering candor, explaining the new rules, describing the finish line, and letting people know that change never ends. By the time he was done, people were no longer afraid of change; they saw it as an opportunity, not a threat.

☐ **Align rewards with the architecture and the operating system.** Rewarding for the right outcomes makes sure that energy is properly directed. Welch knew that for companywide initiatives to succeed, he would have to reinforce their importance at every opportunity (meetings, reviews, and so on). For example, at one point he made 40 percent of a senior manager's bonus contingent upon results achieved with Six Sigma. Review your incentive plan, and make sure that it does what it is supposed to do. If it falls short, tweak the plan so that the greatest rewards go to the greatest contributors.

☐ **Involve everyone.** A company's total energy—and intellect—is enhanced when everyone is asked to contribute. No organization can afford to leave players on the sidelines. Consider those with the softest voices (the ones you hear from the least), and come up with additional projects that encourage their participation. Tell each of them, in your own words, that he or she is too important to be left on the bench for the whole game.

CHAPTER 2

THE 4E LEADER
ENERGIZES

*Energizers inspire, mobilize people to act, and spark others
to perform. They don't engage in turf wars, operate in silos,
or tolerate backbiting behavior.*

The best energizers have an unvarnished, unqualified brand
of enthusiasm. They can get their colleagues charged up
about just about anything. People *respond* to them, and
that response makes them particularly effective. They bring out
the best in people, inject them with confidence, and give *them* the
credit when things go right. They are the organization's confidence
builders. That's why Welch decreed that "the ability to
energize is the ingredient that counts."

Welch also said: "You have no right to be a leader if you don't have
it in your soul to build others. Nothing is worse than a whirling
dervish who bores everyone. You need fertilizer and water."

"Fertilizer and water," it turns out, is Welch's metaphor for effective
leadership. The 4E Leader spreads confidence like gardeners
spread fertilizer. That's why, according to Welch, the most
important thing a leader does is to instill confidence into the
soul of the organization.

One of the keys to sparking others to perform is to make sure that workers are engaged in jobs that challenge and stimulate them. Welch decided early in his own career that dull, monotonous work saps an individual's energy faster than almost anything else. As a result, he set his sights on creating an environment in which people could grow and learn.

Energize with a Few Clear Objectives

Welch said that leadership is the ability to articulate a vision and the ability to get others to *act* on that vision. What does that mean in the context of energizing? It means refraining from micromanaging, and instead giving your people a few clear, simple goals.

The best leaders manage *less,* not more. Bureaucrats whack people with the twin sticks of systems and procedures; *leaders,* by contrast, inspire. In the GE of his early years with the company, Welch decided that he saw far too many of the former and not enough of the latter. "Big corporations are filled with people in bureaucracy," he commented in the early 1990s, "who want to cover things—cover the bases, say they did everything a little bit."

Why instruct managers to focus on only a few clear goals? The reason touches on another key Welch imperative: *simplicity.* Complexity obscures; simplicity cuts right to the heart of the matter. He admired people who were confident enough to use simple words and give simple presentations.

Organizational strategies should also be simple. Welch protégé Robert Nardelli worked for Welch at GE for many years before snaring the top post at retailing giant Home Depot in 2000. In early 2005, Nardelli spoke of the importance of articulating the firm's strategy simply and succinctly:

> *Our strategy for the Home Depot is one page.*
> *Basically, our core purpose is to improve everything*
> *we touch. Underneath that core purpose is a strategy*
> *that talks about enhancing the core, extending the*
> *business and expanding our markets. Now, those three*
> *are kind of chiseled in granite and are timeless.*
> *The economy of those three initiatives ...will serve*
> *us well for decades to come.*

Another aspect of simplicity, as Welch saw it, was *timing*. Things did not need to be "Harvard-tough" all of the time. Employees did not need to be bombarded with multiple complex programs at once, or even in rapid succession. Instead, Welch rolled out his major initiatives one at a time every few years.

For example, in 1996, Welch launched the initiative that would consume him for the next five years: Six Sigma. When he looked for people to lead the charge, GE managers answered the chairman's call in unprecedented numbers, making the GE Six Sigma program the largest corporate initiative ever launched by any company.

Welch is the first to admit that Six Sigma was not invented by GE. (In fact, electronics manufacturer Motorola pioneered it in the United States.) But Welch and GE can be credited with creating a Six Sigma crusade that was unmatched in its scale and scope. Welch is also quick to admit that, at first, he didn't see the potential benefits of Six Sigma, rather he concluded that it was simply another management fad—long on slogans and short on substance.

But his friend and former vice chairman Larry Bossidy convinced Welch that Six Sigma was the real thing. Bossidy promised Welch that if he and GE decided to take the plunge, they could "write the book on quality." Welch was not one to shrink from a challenge; in addition, his own employees were telling him that GE's quality standards were unacceptably low. Typically, he jumped in with both feet.

First, he launched the Six Sigma initiative at his January managers' meeting in Boca Raton. Then, as the program was rolled out, he took every opportunity to hammer the point home. Whether it was in his annual letter to shareowners or in a company speech or a handwritten note to a manager, he constantly drilled away, letting everyone know that this was his top priority.

"In my four decades with GE," Welch wrote in April 1999, "I have never seen a company initiative move so willingly and so rapidly in pursuit of a big idea." The program literally consumed Welch for years. He admitted that he was a bit "unbalanced" on the subject—but he also argued that people need to be "fanatical" if they are going to launch programs like these.

Note, however, that throughout his "unbalanced" pursuit of Six Sigma, Welch kept his company *focused.* Employees at other companies sometimes spoke derisively of the "program of the month" imposed upon them by management; not so at GE. In his 20-plus years at the company's helm, Welch launched a total of only five major initiatives (Globalization, Work-Out, Product Services, Six Sigma, and Digitization).

And just as important to the success of these initiatives was the *way* in which Welch launched them. Yes, he took the lead as the single most vocal and ardent supporter of the latest initiative. But at the same time, he avoided micromanaging. (Leaders manage *less,* not more.)

Welch seldom set rigid agendas for his senior management meetings related to an ongoing initiative. Instead, he preferred to throw

THE 4E LEADER SETS ONLY A FEW CLEAR GOALS

Energizers know that the key to motivating is not to micromanage, but to outline a few general goals and let people run with them. Energizers hire people who have energy—and the ability to energize others.

out a topic or two and ask his direct reports for their best ideas of the last 90 days.

At the same time, he popularized the concept of *informality*, which he brought to every corner of the company: "I may be kidding myself," declared Welch to a reporter, "but going to a CEC meeting for me is like going to a fraternity party and hanging out with my friends."

New Ideas Energize Everyone

Few things got Welch more energized than new ideas. Extrapolating from his own experience, he was convinced that new ideas were the lifeblood of the organization. "The hero is the one with the idea," he once declared. Ideas, learning, training—all contribute to the collective intellect of the organization.

Energizers aren't necessarily the source of ideas; more likely, they encourage others to voice their ideas. They know that few things get people more excited than having one of their ideas lead to an important "win" for the organization.

Conversely, what happens when people are *not* able to contribute their brainpower to the organization? They feel increasingly isolated and not in control of their own destinies. When that happens, most people get into a "reactive" mode, feeling more like victims than like contributors.

Peter Senge's research confirms this: "Many organizations unintentionally encourage the reactive orientation, by keeping most employees out of any meaningful participation in decisions, planning, or learning. With no opportunity to take responsibility themselves, people learn to keep their defenses up, duck blame, and avoid initiative. They are toyed with . . . not by the gods . . . but by those people on the top floor."

In a creative, knowledge-hungry environment, individuals have a much more positive outlook on the world. Instead of attributing blame or feeling victimized, explains Senge, they feel *energized.* They are able and willing to tackle new challenges. They do not feel constrained by yesterday. They work longer and harder, as a "can-do" culture works itself deep into the fabric of the company. And (not incidentally) the leader's vision is enlarged in such an organization, and he or she can devote more time and energy to big-picture issues.

One way to move the organization in this direction is to make sure that there is a mechanism in place for people to contribute new ideas. At GE, one of the main idea-exchanging centers was Crotonville. But Crotonville, as noted earlier, was a *management* training facility.

Through the early years of Welch's tenure, there was no equivalent mechanism available to the nonmanagerial ranks, which made up the vast majority of the company's employees. This is one reason why Welch conceived and launched his "Work-Out" program: to ensure that *all* GE employees had a forum in which to contribute new ideas.

Before Welch became CEO, there was a feeling among top management that the company already had all the answers. As a result of the upheavals launched by Welch, the company stopped feeling smug and started looking for good ideas wherever it could find them:

> *This boundaryless learning culture killed any view that assumed the GE way was the only way, or even the best way. . . . And the operative compulsion is to find out who has the better idea, learn it, and put it into action—fast.*

Welch made it known that there were neither boundaries nor hierarchies when it came to articulating an idea. Everyone could, and *had to*, contribute new ideas. "The quality of an idea does not depend on its altitude in the organization," observed Welch. "An idea can come from any source. So we will search the globe for ideas . . . we have a constant quest to raise the bar, and we get there by constantly talking to others."

> *If you and I and the business leadership of this country can have the self-confidence to let people go— to create an environment where each man and woman who works in our companies can see a clear connection between what he or she does every day, all day, and winning and losing in the real world—we can become productive beyond our wildest dreams.*

The second critical way to energize the organization—beyond searching within the company and around the world for good ideas—is to make sure that the ideas are *acted* upon. The GE operating system, described earlier, was in part designed for this purpose: It was a system for converting ideas into action. Words like *action, speed,* and *pounce* began showing up regularly in Welch's speeches and documents—implying that the hunt didn't end when the quarry came into view.

And once again, Welch walked the talk. For example, when he learned that one of his managers, Lloyd Trotter, had created a matrix that helped promote best practices at the 40 factories under his supervision, Welch couldn't wait to disseminate that knowledge across the company. The "Trotter Matrix" became one of the best-known management tools at GE.

Welch also made sure to pick up great ideas from other companies. In 1991, Welch, like the heads of many other Wal-Mart suppliers, made the trek to Bentonville, Arkansas, to meet with Sam Walton. But Welch was less interested in currying favor with Wal-Mart than in learning how Wal-Mart was combining "high touch from the field with high-tech" at headquarters to stay responsive, even as the company was growing by billions (in sales) every year.

Maybe the lessons wouldn't translate directly (GE was a very different animal from Wal-Mart), but it certainly made sense, as Welch saw it, to try those lessons on for size.

Ideas are everywhere. "I know if I pan this room tonight and talk to everyone here," Welch told a New York audience in 1999, "I'd learn a zillion things about how to do my job better."

The lesson? Make sure that everyone in your shop is constantly monitoring the environment, the marketplace, the competition,

> ## THE 4E LEADER MAKES SURE THAT GOOD IDEAS ARE SURFACED, CELEBRATED, AND ACTED UPON
>
> Make sure that there is a platform through which people can contribute new ideas (e.g., Work-Out), and then celebrate the ideas by spreading them throughout the company. Make sure that the best ideas are *acted* upon, and give credit to those who come up with them.

and so on. Welch said that the operative assumption at his firm was that someone out there had found a better way of doing something. The challenge, then, was to do everything humanly possible to learn what that someone—whoever he or she might be—had learned and then incorporate that knowledge into GE's own playbook.

Sometimes a new idea can come as part of a bigger package—for example, through an alliance or strategic acquisition. For GE, one such idea came as a result of the $6 billion acquisition of RCA in 1986. That acquisition, as it turned out, provided the inspiration and foundation for GE's massive expansion into service businesses.

But acquisitions typically are the sole purview of senior managers. Therefore, they can be only one piece of a much bigger puzzle. The key is to get people at *every* level involved with innovation.

Energizers Excel in Learning Organizations

As discussed in the previous chapter, it is critical to have the right infrastructure (i.e., social systems) in place so that The 4E Leader can succeed. Welch simplified the organization chart. He also "fixed, closed, or sold" troubled businesses. And, as noted earlier, he insisted that all GE businesses be either number 1 or number 2 in their respective markets. (Not surprisingly, word quickly spread across the GE empire that Welch wasn't fond of being number 2.)

Finally, he disposed of those operating units that did not match his vision of the new GE. He described that vision in terms of "three circles": core, technology, and service businesses. As a result of these and other actions, he established a new strategic direction for the company that has stood the test of time to this day.

But all these strategic changes were only the first phase of Welch's revolution, which came to be dubbed the "hardware phase." It was the "software phase"—the rebuilding period that followed all the bloodletting and restructuring and that focused on restoring confidence—that truly energized the organization.

In his book, *Execution,* Larry Bossidy explained that this "social software" is "what brings the corporate hardware to life as a functioning system. . . . The design of structure is obviously important, but it is the software that integrates the organization into a unified, synchronized whole."

Bossidy also pointed out that the "social operating mechanisms"—the meetings, training, e-mails, dialogue, presentations, and so on—were enormously beneficial to GE. One of the reasons was their integrative nature: They broke down walls between jobs and across functions and within hierarchies. They also helped to create new information flows and new working relationships. Finally, they helped to tear down walls between the company and the outside world as well.

GE's social architecture—its energy-filled, high-involvement culture—provided the foundation upon which Welch could fulfill his goal of creating an authentic learning culture. In the early period, Welch used the somewhat stilted phrase "integrated diversity" to embody the sharing of ideas across all of GE's businesses.

Later, he dropped "integrated diversity" in favor of the "learning organization" (or sometimes the "learning company"): "The combination of involving everyone in the game and of responding to this flow of ideas and information turned GE into what we are today—a learning company."

What, exactly, is a learning organization? Charles Handy, author of *The Age of Unreason,* explains that a learning organization "can mean two things. It can mean an organization which learns and/or an organization which encourages learning in its people. It should mean both." At Welch's GE, it did. According to most experts, Welch was the business leader who was most responsible for popularizing the concept of organizational learning in the 1990s and beyond.

THE 4E LEADER GIVES EQUAL WEIGHT TO STRUCTURAL DECISIONS AND SOCIAL MECHANISMS

Welch started his revolution at GE by focusing on the structure: fixing businesses, controlling expenses, eliminating management layers. But he also set his sights on creating a performance-based culture. He understood that both structural and social factors play an important role in developing a culture of winning. Neglecting either could leave your organization vulnerable.

Performance Reviews in a Learning Organization

One of the key distinguishing characteristics of a learning organization is the interactive nature of its performance reviews. In *The Fifth Discipline Fieldbook*, Peter Senge and his team wrote of the importance of engaging employees in an interactive dialogue at annual review time. Unfortunately (according to Senge), most managers do not engage in such two-way conversations.

To energize employees, make a habit of asking these types of questions at review time:

- What do you want to achieve in the next 12 months? What do you want to achieve in the ensuing few years?

- What is it in the organization that will help you to make your goals? What roadblocks will interfere with your progress?

- What else do you need from the organization to help you accomplish your objectives?

- What things do I—your manager—do that hinder your efforts?

- And last but not least, according to Senge: What is your pattern of failure? What danger signals should I look for ahead of time so that I know to come talk to you and help you?

By engaging your employees in this type of dialogue, you will learn a great deal about what makes your people tick. You will learn what energizes them—and what stands in the way of their being energized. Most likely, patterns will emerge, which you can interpret and act upon.

One key to success in this effort is to *encourage candor by being candid yourself.* People are more likely to put themselves on the line with you if you go first.

Another key to success in this effort is to *hold interactive dialogues frequently.* These dialogues should not be a once-a-year event. (Indeed, some business scholars argue that such a discussion is impractical when compensation issues are on the table or about to be on the table.)

In the best-run companies, informal, meaningful dialogue goes on every day and in every corner of the organization. The 4E Leader understands this, encouraging consistent, candid dialogue throughout the organization.

Welch did not wait for annual review time to engage his managers in a meaningful discussion about the company, the employees, and GE's latest business initiatives. He loved to engage in extended, free-flowing discussions with managers at Crotonville. He would

THE 4E LEADER CONSISTENTLY ENGAGES EMPLOYEES IN A TWO-WAY DIALOGUE

If you take a genuine interest in your employees, you will be rewarded with empathy, trust, and a more motivated team. It is important for you to understand your employees' hopes, frustrations, and so on. You may learn what's preventing your group from progressing to the next level, as well as identify those success levers that may help them to get there.

often send participants a handwritten note ahead of the session, letting them know what topics were likely to be covered. In his memoir, Welch wrote that he would ask managers the following:

What were their most frequent sources of frustration?

What would they change about the company if they could?

How is the latest companywide initiative going? How would they "accelerate it in your area, your business, and the company"?

Energize with "One Currency"

By the mid-1990s, Welch could credibly argue that he had achieved many of his initial goals. Crotonville was turning out impressive young business leaders, GE's operating system (its systematic meetings and reviews) was schooling thousands of employees in critical initiatives like globalization and product services, and the company's shared values appeared to be reinforcing its overriding priorities.

But Welch knew that there was more hard work to be done. The last piece of the "energizing" puzzle was the reward system. Typically, executives receive some combination of salary, bonus, and stock options. Options tend to be favored more heavily (and distributed more widely) in start-ups, high-tech ventures, and other risky propositions. Old Economy companies, by contrast, tend to restrict options grants to senior managers, a few hand-picked executives, and the companies' outside directors.

Welch decided to borrow a page from the upstarts. He established a system whereby more and more managers received stock options every year. This, he was convinced, gave everyone a strong incentive to work as one. "At GE," declared Welch in *Jack,* "there is only one currency: GE stock. There are different amounts of it for different levels of performance, but everyone's life raft is tied to the same boat."

Welch hastened to add that "one culture, one set of values, one currency" didn't necessarily translate into "one style." But his main point remained: Managers who worked for him needed to believe that they were all on the same life raft, and that there was only one currency worth having.

Why was Welch's "one currency" doctrine so important? The answer has two parts. First, it reinforced his "shared values" doctrine—that is, the importance of having all GE employees and managers march to the same tune. And this, in turn, helped Welch to boost productivity across *all* of GE's businesses despite the diversity of the company's vast portfolio.

Without productivity growth, it is possible to lose in twenty-four months businesses that took half a century to build. Productivity growth is essential to industrial survival.

Welch did not implement Six Sigma in only his manufacturing businesses, for example, or launch Work-Out in only one of the company's three strategic "rings." He was convinced that the concepts had universal applicability, given the right foundation and the right cultural context.

In fact, one of the most valuable aspects of the Welch doctrine is its general applicability. Many of its component parts can be put to good use in almost any organization, regardless of its size or

THE 4E LEADER IS COMMITTED
TO BUILDING A ONE-RAFT,
ONE-CURRENCY ORGANIZATION

While Welch used differentiation as a key management tool, he was careful to build a company that was governed by a single set of values. He also made sure that all managers had the incentive to make the company successful by paying all of them with the same "currency."

industry, as long as the leader of the organization has found ways to "energize" that organization.

We should recall that Jack Welch was labeled a heretic, and worse, during his first tumultuous decade at the helm of GM. Welch lived with his critics during that first decade and effectively silenced them in his second. The results of his many initiatives were indisputable: The company was chalking up incredible results. A $10,000 investment in GE when Welch started would be worth more than $367,000 before he stepped down, or 250 percent of the increase of the average Standard & Poor's (S&P) stock during the same period.

Once GE started to win, *really* win, people began to find a great deal to get excited about in Welch's approach. One thing that many of these would-be emulators didn't pick up on was the synergistic relationship between *energizers* and *learning organizations*. In a learning organization, energizers thrive. They spark others to learn, improve, execute, and win. Why? Because the social systems to achieve these vital objectives are in place.

And, at the same time, learning organizations benefit hugely from the presence of energizers. Indeed, if Welch's GE is any indicator, the learning organization can be built only by a highly placed, determined energizer. Welch's learning organization was built atop the shoulders of several key leaders who turned out to be effective energizers in their own right. Home Depot's Robert Nardelli was an energizer that impressed his former boss. In looking back at his first years in his new post, Nardelli took pride in how he had rejuvenated a company that had fallen on hard times. In early 2005, he explained how hitting all the right notes creates an organization of motivated, loyal employees:

> *We've really tried to create a very transparent organization focusing heavily on alignment, focusing heavily on creating a culture that allows people to learn, and then to launch…. In four years we have made tremendous accomplishments finally measured in our employee of choice survey. Our scores are twenty points better than the industry norm.*

When employees are satisfied, attests Nardelli, they understand the company strategy better and are far more likely to recommend the company to a friend or colleague.

Energize with a New, Big Thing

Let's look again at the RCA acquisition, which was introduced earlier in the context of turning up new ideas. There is another way to look at major acquisitions: as a way to energize an entire organization. Welch called it the "quantum leap."

GE and RCA originally had been part of the same company, but in 1933, the Justice Department broke the company up to promote a more competitive marketplace. Now, half a century later, the wheel had turned, and Welch saw an opportunity in a less regulated marketplace for GE to acquire RCA and its "crown jewel": the National Broadcasting Company (NBC).

Welch knew full well that after a company goes through the kind of massive restructuring that he had imposed on GE, morale tends to plummet. But he also knew that a well-planned coup— a quantum leap—tends to lift spirits and has the potential to energize the company and unite it around a common cause.

Although many questioned the logic of what was still perceived as a far-flung manufacturing conglomerate purchasing a television network, Welch knew that the deal had the potential to energize the entire company.

In his memoir, he described the effect that the merger announcement had on his management team: "The deal changed the atmosphere." Welch then described the scene at the annual managers' meeting in Boca Raton: "I remember walking up to the stage for

THE 4E LEADER LOOKS FOR THE QUANTUM LEAP

What bold stroke could you make that not only would enhance your company's competitive position but also would energize your workforce by demonstrating that they're part of a dynamic, winning team? A cautionary note: Most studies suggest that major acquisitions often do relatively little to increase shareholder value. A quantum leap is a quantum leap only if it works.

the opening session. . . . All of a sudden, some 500 people in the room stood up in a spontaneous ovation. RCA became the kickstart to a new era."

Energize on Strength

Jack Welch was a "natural," someone who knew intuitively what others had to learn. He understood that one of the keys to effective leadership is to build on strengths—particularly on the strengths of the individual. Several recent books have extolled the virtues of energizing on strength.

In their noteworthy book, *Now, Discover Your Strengths,* Gallup researchers Marcus Buckingham and Donald Clifton emphasize the importance of an organization's leading with its strengths. "You can't lead a strengths revolution," the authors assert, "if you don't know how to find, name and develop your own."

Of course, management scholars have long argued for building on strengths. Once again, Peter Drucker proves to have been the pioneer. In his best work, 1954's *The Practice of Management,* he wrote: "One cannot do anything with what one cannot do. One cannot achieve anything with what one does not do. One can only build on strength. One can achieve only by doing."

But Welch, typically, took the notion of building on strengths an important step further. He believed that tapping strengths not only set the organization on the right path but also *energized* it. Batteries are not drawn down when you build on strengths; they are recharged. This was the theory behind both the "hardware" and "software" phases of his reinvention of GE. In a sense, the hardware phase (the restructuring of the portfolio) was an exercise in creating energy by freeing up underproductive assets.

Equally, the software phase (rebuilding systems and corporate morale) aimed at energizing people.

Work-Out, as noted, was launched on the premise that the strength of the individual trumps everything else. "My view of the 1990s is based on the liberation of the workplace," Welch wrote. "If you want to get the benefit of everything employees have, you've got to free them, make everybody a participant. Everybody has to know everything, so they can make the right decisions by themselves."

To build on strengths, consider performing a "strengths audit" of your business on both the "hardware" and the "software" fronts—that is, its competitive position in the marketplace and the quality and suitability of its human capital. The following "large questions" are a good place to start:

1. What is the sustainable advantage that will help our business succeed on both a short-term and a long-term basis?

2. If the answer is unsatisfactory or not immediately clear, what competencies, technology, and so on does our business have to acquire to provide a sustainable advantage?

3. Are our people strong enough to do the hard work ahead of us? List the key individuals on a sheet of paper, and jot down the five most important strengths of each of them. Who is the best communicator? Who is the best closer? Who sparks others to perform? Who is the hardest worker?

4. Are our people in the right jobs? Sometimes a great person is stuck in the wrong job. Is each of your direct reports performing a job that plays to his or her strengths? If not, figure out

> ## THE 4E LEADER BUILDS ON THE STRENGTH OF THE ORGANIZATION AND THE INDIVIDUAL
>
> If you were framing out a house, you'd worry about two things at once: the quality of the (emerging) structure and the quality of the crew that was building that structure. Great corporations are built in the same way: on many levels at once, with knowledge from one level informing decisions on another.

a longer-term plan to reconfigure the organization, with the proviso that the business must continue to operate in the short term.

Energize on a Stretch Vision

Before Welch, GE lived modestly (despite its standing as one of the largest industrial corporations in the United States). Welch's predecessors aimed for single-digit growth (usually in the low to middle single digits), which was seen as befitting an established industrial firm. As long as the company grew faster than the U.S. economy as a whole, that was enough. GE was one of a number of companies that were referred to as "GNP companies," those whose fortunes tended to mirror the gross national product.

Welch's goal was far more ambitious. He aimed for double-digit growth, and he achieved it, year in and year out. He was so successful, in fact, that by the 1990s the stock market assigned a "Welch premium" to GE's shares, which meant that the company's shares sold at 40 to 50 times earnings for most of his GE tenure (the average large U.S. company typically sells at about half that).

Welch felt that it was far better to shoot for the moon and fall short by a little than to hit easy targets. In 1979, in a letter Welch wrote to convince then-CEO Reg Jones that he was ready for the job, Welch argued with rough eloquence that those who worked under him "gained increased self-respect and self-confidence from accomplishing more than they previously thought possible."

He used an interesting phrase to describe this phenomenon. He was "selling runway," he wrote—the "capacity to grow, something I've always looked for in every appointment I have made." Then he underscored the point, adding that he "always bet on runway."

In other words, if you put a little more runway in front of someone and encourage them to take off—at high speed, in a new direction—good things happen. You stretch that person's vision.

As CEO, Welch insisted that his leaders do the same: "We have found that by reaching for what appears to be impossible, we often actually do the impossible; and even when we don't quite make it, we inevitably wind up doing much better than we would have done."

Welch considered the budget process to be the antithesis of "selling runway" and cultivating stretch visions. Typically, managers lock themselves up in a room for two days. One bean counter says "nine"; the other says "seven." Eventually, they compromise on "eight," pat themselves on the back for a job well done, and get back to their real jobs.

What could be more *moronic*, Welch asked? Locking managers in a room—isolated from the customers, products, and new ideas that Welch considered to be the lifeblood of the company—was a horrendous waste of precious resources. It was an energy drain and a vision shrinker.

It was much better to aim for a heroic twelve and hit ten than to aim for an easy eight. Stretch targets motivate and energize. Budgets grow caution and inward thinking; they sap life out of the company. "Decimal points are a bore," Welch once remarked.

Any manager who has lived through the budget process (even the most dyed-in-the-wool bean counter) takes the point. Individuals rise to the challenges that are put in front of them, and the bigger the better. John F. Kennedy set one of the most celebrated stretch goals in recent history when he declared (in 1961) that the United States would "send a man to the moon and return him safely to the earth by the end of the decade." It was a totally unrealistic goal, in light of the then-available technology. No matter. "We do these things not because they are easy," he added, "but because they are hard." And in the summer of 1969, that stretch vision was realized.

THE 4E LEADER AIMS HIGH, ASKING MORE OF PEOPLE THAN THEY THEMSELVES BELIEVE THEY CAN DELIVER

If you allow the system to set low expectations, you surely will get them. Set stretch targets, and ask your team to rise to the challenge. Many teams will respond when asked to perform seemingly impossible tasks. Reward them when they do—and also when they miss by a respectable margin. A "stretch failure" is often better than an easy success.

ARE YOU AN ENERGIZER?

Take a few minutes to answer the following questions about you and your management style. In keeping with the Welch themes, this is an informal exercise. However, it should give you some idea as to how you rate on the second E:

1. In assigning goals to your team, do you tend to limit them to a few clear objectives?

2. Do you consistently energize your colleagues by articulating a vision and getting them to carry it out?

3. Do you make it clear to everyone who reports to you that contributing new ideas is part of their job?

4. Do you reward or celebrate the best ideas (give the person accolades, send handwritten notes, and so on)?

5. Do you make a habit of engaging your direct reports in a two-way dialogue?

6. Does your organization live by a "one-raft" philosophy (e.g., use company stock or stock options as a primary reward for the best managers)?

7. Do you periodically review and prune all businesses and/or product lines? That is, do you ask yourself Drucker's question: "If you weren't already in the business or market, would you enter it today, knowing what you know?"

8. Do you focus on people's strengths rather than on their weaknesses? That is, do you put people in the posts where they can do the most good rather than putting them where they can do the least harm?

9. Do you lead by example by living the values of the firm?

10. Do you set stretch goals rather than aiming for small, incremental gains?

If you responded in the affirmative to eight or more, consider you and your organization to be ahead of the curve.

Any score below five is a bad sign. Chances are that morale is suffering and your unit is not operating nowhere near its potential.

A tally between five and eight means that your firm is a "tweener" and that there is some room for improvement.

The 4E Leader To-Do List

☐ **Create a systematic method for learning and implementing Best Practices.** Welch created a new mind-set inside GE, letting everyone know that arrogance and complacency would not be tolerated. He institutionalized learning. Over the years, GE studied many companies to learn new things, including IBM, Ford, and Hewlett-Packard.

☐ **Bring informality to the workplace.** Welch once said that the untold chapter of the GE story is that GE is an informal place. He took off his tie and blew away much of the company's traditional pomp and circumstance. When *Time* sent a photographer, Welch declined to put on a jacket. "I don't want to look stuck up," he said.

☐ **Identify the next big, new thing.** Welch knew that a big deal or acquisition (such as sewing up all broadcast rights to the Olympics through 2008 for $2.3 billion) has the potential to energize the entire company and create unanticipated opportunities. Figure out what the next big thing is in your industry, and commit resources to making it happen.

☐ **Celebrate the best ideas.** Welch said that one of the company's great strengths was its ability to celebrate the best ideas. That's what he did when one of his managers created a better mousetrap (e.g., the Trotter Matrix). Energize by making sure that the credit goes to the people who come up with the best ideas.

☐ **Set bigger goals.** Welch knew that the key to achieving big things was to think bigger. If you are at 5, it is better to aim for 12 than for 5.8. The former GE chairman declared decimal points a bore and claimed that he never fired anyone for missing a stretch goal.

☐ **Beef up the incentive plan.** Don't be afraid to beef up the incentive plan by including more and more managers in that plan. But be sure that you are rewarding people for the precise contributions that the organization requires for success.

CHAPTER 3

THE 4E LEADER
HAS *EDGE*

*Individuals with edge have a competitive spirit
and know the value of speed. They're confident;
they know when to green-light or red-light
a project or acquisition. They don't get
paralyzed by paradox.*

Welch loved to talk sports and business, and he could almost always be counted upon to come up with a sports analogy to fit a specific business situation. Those analogies are very much in evidence when he speaks of the third E: edge.

"The market is rewarding you like Super Bowl winners or Olympic gold medalists," he once commented. "I know I have such athletes reporting to me. Can you put your team against my team? Are you proud of everyone who reports to you? If you aren't, you can't win."

To Welch, business is about *winning:* winning in the marketplace, winning customers, winning new business, winning for shareholders. Welch's number 1, number 2 edict certainly illustrates his competitive nature. When he signed a $4 million contract to

"AMERICA'S MAYOR" SHOWS HIS EDGE

A political leader who had edge in abundance was "America's Mayor," Rudolph Giuliani (who happens to be a Welch fan). Giuliani showed that edge on September 11, 2001, the day of the tragic terrorist attacks on New York. Just months from retirement as the city's mayor, he could have hunkered down, issuing commands from an undisclosed location.

Instead, he was everywhere at once (most often at Ground Zero), helping, guiding, *leading*. Even his harshest critics applauded him that day. But what they probably didn't know is how he had prepared himself for leadership.

Giuliani urges others to "prepare relentlessly." He says he learned early on never to "assume a damn thing," and he followed his own advice. For example, before being elected mayor, he was concerned that he would come to the job not fully prepared. So he put together a tutorial on being mayor, including a series of seminars designed to help educate him on those aspects of the mayor's job that he knew the least well.

Those sessions, he later wrote, not only provided the knowledge he needed but also afforded him the chance to think through how he would perform in various situations. He argued that leaders should take all the time they have to make the best decisions, but they should start weighing alternatives *now*, not days from now.

He may have been what Drucker would call a "natural," but he took nothing for granted and left little to chance. He prepared for leadership relentlessly and held himself accountable to tough standards. All these factors converged—to New York's and the nation's benefit—on the one day that they mattered most.

write his second book—a prescriptive, "how-to" management book—he simply called it *Winning*.

But Welch's approach to winning was far from simplistic or one-dimensional. He knew that the path to winning is sometimes a winding one. He understood that managing less was managing more, that the key to success was producing more with less. And he knew that he had to manage *many* businesses while imposing a *single* vision, that of a learning, boundaryless organization.

Embracing complexity and paradox while still maintaining clarity of vision and *edge* is a difficult balancing act. Welch understood that, and he achieved it better than most.

Maintaining Edge in the Face of Paradox

Many of Welch's early moves confirmed what he had suspected from the beginning: that reinventing a company required many actions that tugged in contradictory directions. Most immediately, he had to tear down in order to build. He had to find a way of "managing long term while 'eating' short term." Welch did a great job of balancing the two, which is one of the reasons he was so successful.

One way he did so was to cut costs ruthlessly. In his first five years at the helm of GE, Welch cut one out of every four people on the GE payroll (118,000 people, including 37,000 people from businesses that were divested).

But there were countervailing currents as well. At the same time that Welch was cutting deeply into the payroll, he was spending millions on what he called "nonproductive" things. He upgraded the Crotonville facility, and he built a gym, a guesthouse, and a conference center for the Fairfield headquarters.

Understandably, people inside and outside the company objected to these priorities. How could Welch justify spending millions ($75 million, to be exact) on Crotonville and the Fairfield headquarters while cutting so many jobs? Welch heard and understood these protests, but he was undeterred.

This was simply a paradox of business: You have to shrink in order to grow; you have to give things up in order to gain things. By eliminating jobs and closing unproductive factories (difficult as those moves were for the people who were directly affected), he was creating the means to reinvigorate the places that would spark the company's transformation. If GE could not attract, train, and retain "A players" (which is how Welch referred to top performers), the company would fall farther and farther behind in the competitive marketplace.

It took some time for many to see the logic of Welch's actions, but eventually they came around. Again, the results were irrefutable. By the late 1980s, all the key metrics of productivity were up significantly: profit margins, inventory turns, and so on. By managing contradictory tugs within the organization (which were at times quite powerful) while still defending his vision, Welch demonstrated that he was a manager with edge—someone who didn't shy away from the tough decisions. He and his team of consultants summed it up like this:

Paradox is a way of life. You must function collectively as one company and individually as many businesses at the same time. For us, leadership means leading while being led, producing more output with less input.

MANAGERS WITH THE THIRD E KNOW HOW TO MANAGE PARADOX

Welch understood that many apparent contradictions in business resolve in the face of a larger vision—and may not be contradictory at all. He knew how to manage "hard" and "soft"—that is, how to cut some expenses drastically while boosting spending in other areas. Ultimately, business is all about taking care of the short term while providing for the long term. Many people are prepared to do one or the other, but managers with edge find ways to do both simultaneously.

Win Through Differentiation

Welch's focus on people and the social mechanisms confirmed his commitment to developing the best and the brightest at GE. He knew that he could not do it alone. He understood that the key to genuine transformation was "getting the people part right." Here is how Jim Collins phrased this challenge in *Good to Great*: "The good-to-great leaders began the transformation by first getting the right people on the bus (and the wrong people off the bus), and then figured out where to drive it."

GE already had a well-earned reputation for its commitment to management development. Welch's predecessor, Reg Jones, had spent seven years searching for his successor. (Ultimately, Welch would demonstrate the same intensity when selecting his own successor, Jeffrey Immelt.) But the real story of GE's success in developing leaders during Welch's tenure was to be found not in the chairman's office, but all along the GE food chain.

How did Welch do it? First, he didn't do it overnight. Leadership development takes years rather than weeks or months. Some of the tools he used have already been referred to: establishing the GE values (and making adherence to them mandatory), implementing Work-Out, and establishing candor and trust through meetings and reviews via the GE operating system.

But he also *differentiated*—in part based on his personal experience with the company. It is a story full of might-have-beens: Some four decades earlier, a brash twenty-something maverick named Jack Welch resigned from GE when he was given the same "lousy" $1,000 raise as everybody else. He was livid.

Here he was chalking up victory after victory, and the company didn't think enough of him to give him a better raise than everyone else? It took no small amount of coaxing to convince Welch to change his mind and stay. That lesson stayed with Welch for decades, and it taught him a good deal about the importance of differentiation and leadership. As Welch put it:

> *Differentiation is all about being extreme, rewarding the best and weeding out the ineffective. Rigorous differentiation delivers real stars and stars build great businesses.*

Welch's affinity for differentiation tells us a good deal about his larger philosophy. He says that we spend the first 20 years of our life being differentiated, from first-grade quizzes through college entrance exams. Why should we stop differentiating when we enter the working world?

Critics have challenged Welch on this point time and again. To answer the critics, Welch turns to a baseball analogy: "Just look at the way baseball teams pay 20-game winning pitchers and 40-plus

THE 4E LEADER RETAINS THE A'S

Leaders with edge understand that genuine management talent is rare. They "hug" their best people, giving them the best raises, the most sought-after promotions, the most generous stock options, and so on. Sometime you don't know how valuable someone is until you lose him or her, and the cost of regaining what just walked out the door is almost incalculable. Leaders with edge seldom have to find out.

home run hitters." Welch says that the box scores demonstrate clearly just how valuable these "A" players are to their teams, and he likens them to A players in a corporate setting. If you want them to play with edge, says Welch, you have to differentiate—which includes paying the most to the best.

Peter Drucker wrote that the most costly resource in any organization is its management team. Welch understood this intuitively. At his urging, the company made a systematic effort to retain the identified A's. When the company *lost* an A, a postdeparture postmortem was conducted to figure out why—and in many cases, someone was held accountable for that loss.

How successful was GE at keeping its best people? Under Welch, the company lost less than 1 percent of its A's each year.

Leadership and the Vitality Curve

The 4E Leader knows how to make the tough calls, particularly when it comes to the "life-and-death decisions": hiring, firing, and promoting. Few companies put more time into these vital decisions than GE. Welch differentiated between A, B, and C players. As noted previously, A's were the stars; however, B's made up the biggest category, the nucleus of the company. The C's, finally, were underperformers. They missed their goals and/or did not energize. In many cases, they attempted to lead by control or intimidation rather than by the strength of their vision.

At GE, managers had to differentiate by placing all their direct reports into one of three categories:

- The top 20 percent

- The vital 70 percent

- The bottom 10 percent

GE (and other companies with similar programs) called this three-tiered system the "vitality curve." While these categories do not translate directly into A's, B's, and C's, they come close enough to use as a general guideline.

At GE, A's got stock options and generous raises. Most B's also received options. In fact, 100 percent of the strongest-performing group, "role models," received stock options, as did 100 percent of the next best group, called "strong performers" (both A groups), while 50 to 60 percent of the "highly valued" B players also received options.

This represented a tremendous sea of change. Before Welch became CEO, only a handful of top executives (and outside directors) at GE received options. By the time he retired, more than 30,000 GE managers had received options. Welch made millionaires out of hundreds of the managers he considered the company's very best.

Who received stock options at GE?

100 percent of "role models" (A's)

100 percent of "strong performers" (A's)

50 to 60 percent of "highly valued" (B's)

What about the bottom 10 percent? Welch's rulebook dictated that the bottom 10 percent be fired every year—*no matter what.* It was one of Welch's most controversial tenets. How could he talk about building a confident, boundaryless organization and still fire 10 percent of his people every year?

Once again, Welch was comfortable with these contradictory tugs. This was the kind of thing that a leader with edge *did.* He or she made the gut-wrenching decisions—according to a clear set of rules—and moved forward. Along the way, Welch also argued that getting rid of people who aren't cutting it is a lot better than feigning praise and keeping them in the wrong jobs for years. That kind of "false kindness," Welch argued, only hampered a person later in his or her career.

What if a manager simply couldn't do it—couldn't fire the C's or make similar kinds of difficult decisions? Welch was unyielding. He wrote that those who couldn't rid the company of C's "soon found *themselves* in the C category."

Welch also recognized that it is much easier to find and fire the C's the first time around, since every "unpruned" organization has some "dead wood." The elimination of this kind of clear non-performers, Welch argued, gives managers a chance to get tough and to get edge. The second time around, of course, it's much harder. After the second year, it becomes a form of torture. By then, all the obvious choices have been fired, and managers go to great lengths to avoid firing people they like.

But the best leaders, those who are rich in edge, reach down into themselves and find a way to do it. They understand that there are few things as important as having the best people in the key posts.

Author Jim Collins makes the same point (arrived at from a slightly different direction) in *Good to Great*: "Who questions come before 'what' decisions, before vision, before strategy, before organization structure, before tactics. First *who*, then *what*."

There are shades of Welch in Collins' pronouncements. The key, says Collins, is *to face reality when making people decisions*. If you are not sure about a job applicant, listen to your gut, and don't offer him or her the job. Also, don't shrink from making changes. Remove anyone who does not measure up. And last, put your best people where the opportunities are the greatest. Put slightly differently, don't waste talent by having them put out fires all day.

The "Edge" of an Upstart

Welch never stopped talking about making GE ultracompetitive ("the world's most competitive enterprise"). But GE's very bigness—its scale, scope, and geographic reach—risked putting the company at a disadvantage. Welch felt that from this perspective, small companies often had an edge. They understood what Welch called the "penalty of hesitation in the marketplace." Smaller firms are more resilient, more adaptive, and more capable of moving

THE 4E LEADER USES A DIFFERENTIATION SYSTEM TO KEEP THE BEST AND WEED OUT THE WORST

GE had three categories in its curve: the top 20 percent, the middle 70 percent, and the bottom 10 percent. Of course, multiple variations upon this model also could work. Work with your senior human resouces (HR) manager to come up with a system tailored to the needs of your own department or organization. For example, you might decide on a four-tiered system: a 10/20/60/10 system (corresponding to A/B+/B/C). This system has the potential for identifying the next generation of A's in the B+ group.

quickly. This is why Welch's ideal organization was "a big company body" with a "small company soul."

As a rule, Welch despised things that moved slowly. When asked to look back on his career and say what he would have done differently, he responded that he would have done pretty much everything the same, only *faster*. Why? "Bureaucracy is terrified by speed and hates simplicity," he explained. "It fosters defensiveness, intrigue, sometimes meanness. Those who are trapped in it . . . can't be passionate, and . . . won't win."

Welch delivered those words to an audience in San Francisco at about the same time that he was introducing Work-Out in the late 1980s. These oft-cited phrases tell us a great deal about his mind-set. He hated anything that *slowed the company down:* too many management layers, too much arrogance in the executive ranks, and perhaps worse of all, a feeling of entitlement.

85

Based on Welch's example, there are many things managers in large organizations can do to help their organization get faster and work off some of the bureaucratic fat:

■ *Set up small units or cross-functional teams to tackle vital projects.* The 4E Leader doesn't wait for the memo explaining why upstarts have eaten the company's lunch. When Welch feared that the dot-coms were coming to steal GE market share, for example, he set up separate units called "DYB," or "destroy your business," to devise new business models before his virtual competitors could. (In this case, as it turned out, he needn't have worried; most of the upstarts were no match for GE's vaunted infrastructure.)

■ *Swing for the fences.* Welch urged managers to go for the "quantum leap" rather than play it safe. Even in his final years as CEO, he was not afraid to make the biggest gamble of his career: the $45 billion acquisition of technology company Honeywell (eventually blocked by regulators). Rather than incremental or small, measured steps, once, every so often, try for something much bigger or grander. Encourage your direct reports to do the same, and make sure that you don't punish them for failure.

■ *Eliminate "speed bumps" and other productivity barriers.* Think of the last time your organization experienced a serious defeat or setback. Face reality by identifying the possible causes: Was it because a manager dropped the ball? Was it the result of a poorly conceived organizational structure that paralyzed decision making? Was it because everyone was too polite (or dysfunctional) to articulate the problem before it was too late? Whatever it was, purge the company of this and other productivity-killing cancers.

Edge and Growth

As noted, Welch devoted enormous amounts of time and energy to fixing his company's "hardware" and "software." He cut costs relentlessly (including the payroll), and he looked for ways to create synergies and economies across his numerous operating units.

When Welch took over, GE had revenues of about $25 billion. When he stepped down, GE was a $130 billion company. But one of GE's best-kept secrets is that organic growth under Welch averaged *under 10 percent per year.* What explains the huge differential? It was the torrid pace of acquisitions in the Welch era that helped fuel the GE growth engine.

Why a discussion of acquisitions in this chapter on edge? Because, as the figures just given show, playing by the existing rules—even playing *hardball* by the existing rules—is rarely sufficient to make a quantum leap, especially for a huge, established company like GE. Welch sized up the problem and simply changed the rules of the game. He brought edge to the new game. In doing so, he reversed a century of tradition that had eschewed acquisitions in favor of organic growth.

The life-or-death decisions can't be ducked. They need to be tackled head-on by leaders with edge. The Drucker questions are the first order of business: *What is our business? What should it be? Do we have the resources to execute the strategy?* Leaders with edge, says Welch, know how to say yes or no and "avoid the maybes."

Under Welch, GE made an astounding *1,200-plus* acquisitions. It's all too easy to let one's eye slide over that figure, even in italics:

more than a thousand companies vetted, purchased, and assimilated (and probably a much larger number left on the table, for one reason or another).

The press focused on the "one that got away": Honeywell, whose proposed acquisition by GE in 2000 was blocked by European regulators for antitrust reasons. But more than a thousand *didn't* get away, and the large majority of Welch's acquisitions were hugely successful. It is a testament to GE's leaders—and not just Welch, obviously—that they could sustain and act on their vision successfully across this enormous gambit of business activity. It is strong evidence that there was "edge" fairly deep into GE's leadership ranks.

How did they do it? How did Welch and GE figure out which companies to acquire? Welch said that there were four key questions that every manager must ask when evaluating any potential acquisition:

1. Is the target company accretive to earnings?

2. Can we manage it?

3. Is there a fit between cultures?

4. Can we grow the business?

Those four basic questions appear simple enough, but of course, it is almost always more complicated. Answers to these questions are necessarily interpretations. Determining cultural fit is often the thorniest question, since it is a very hard call to make prior to merging two companies. And many managers have learned the hard way that an ill-fated merger can kill productivity, devastate morale, and bog the company down for years.

MORE MERGER AND ACQUISITION (M&A) INSIGHTS FROM A CEO WITH EDGE

John Chambers, the CEO of Cisco Systems, is a self-proclaimed Welch fan. (The respect runs both ways; Welch once invited Chambers to address his troops at a GE managers' meeting.) Chambers employed Welch's number 1, number 2 strategy in managing Cisco's product lines, and this played a major role in how he acquired and grew the company.

While Cisco has not regained its vaunted place as the Internet darling of Wall Street, Chambers survived. He did it by making the tough calls. In the wake of the dot-com meltdown, he cut almost 10,000 jobs, wrote off $2 billion in inventory, and pruned Cisco's product line by 20 percent. This helped Cisco boost net income to an all-time high in the post-NASDAQ/Internet stock crash of the early 2000s.

Chambers, a manager with enough edge to weather nasty downturns, also has an impressive acquisitions record. In the midst of Cisco's greatest acquisition binge, Chambers divulged his criteria for evaluating acquisition targets:

1. A common vision

2. Short-term wins

3. Long-term strategic advantage

4. A "good chemistry match"

5. Geographic proximity (particularly for large acquisitions)

THE 4E LEADER DEVELOPS AN ACQUISITION STRATEGY AND STICKS WITH IT

It is easy to let ego interfere with decision making, particularly when it comes to acquisitions. The key is to create your own criteria and stick to them. Remember that the corporate graveyard is full of managers who sought bigness for its own sake. It's not always the size of an organization that makes it successful.

ASSESS YOUR "EDGE" QUOTIENT

Do you have edge? It is almost always easier to assess others than it is to assess ourselves. However, it is always best to live by Welch's "face reality" mantra. Take a few minutes to quickly answer the following 10 questions:

1. Do you make most decisions in a timely manner, even the tough ones?

2. Do you tend to tackle problems head-on?

3. Do you come to work each day ready to rewrite your agenda if the situations warrant it?

4. Do you deal well with change?

5. Are you a proactive manager; that is, do you routinely identify new opportunities, new markets, and so on?

6. Do you remove nonperformers?

7. Do you take calculated risks?

8. Do you encourage your direct reports to take risks, and do you give some sort of positive feedback, even when things do not go as planned?

9. When one of your direct reports is not getting the job done, do you look him or her in the eye and tell the truth?

10. Do you take responsibility/ownership for problems that arise on your watch?

If you answered yes to at least seven of these questions, chances are that you are a manager with edge. If you answered yes to five or fewer, then you have a way to go. Some organizations do a better job than others of nurturing managers with edge. For instance, if your boss blames you for taking a risk that does not work out, then you are likely to take the same approach with *your* direct reports. Focus on improving those things that are within your control. If you feel inadequate in the edge department, seek opportunities in professional development.

The 4E Leader To-Do List

☐ **Hire nuanced leaders who can live with ambiguity.** Given the current pace of change and complexity, your organization will achieve better results with managers who understand the new environment. To gauge an individual's competence in this area, you will need to develop at least a few questions to ask new applicants—ones that will reveal how well the applicant does with ambiguity/paradox.

☐ **Use differentiation as a management tool.** Workers and managers are not all created equal. While some deny this tough reality, exercising what Welch called "false kindness,"

The 4E Leader knows that keeping the A's and firing the C's is one of the best ways to build a winning business.

☐ **Develop the reflexes of an upstart.** Larger companies are often at a disadvantage, particularly when it comes to making decisions. Challenge yourself and your colleagues to do things faster. Make a list of the unnecessary steps, forms, and approvals needed to get something important done. Make sure that your folks know their customers as well as the grocer in a corner general store knows his or hers. If your people do not know their customers, really know them, they may be taking them for granted. Your rivals will not, and will do everything they can to lure those customers away. Spend time with your key customers, and make sure that every one of your direct reports does the same.

☐ **"Short-circuit" the system.** It's often not enough to eradicate performance barriers. Remember that it is often easier to ask forgiveness than to ask permission. Sometimes you have to defy the "old way" in order to come up with a better way. Pick your battles. The goal is to show how things can get done better and faster with less red tape. Make sure that everyone knows what you are trying to do. Total transparency is a prerequisite, so that your motives will never be called into question. If the crusade is the right one, and you succeed (and nothing succeeds like success), then your actions may help your firm to develop faster reflexes.

☐ **Use "edge thinking" to rewrite the rules of the game.** Welch evidently came into his job hoping to make the huge GE engine run better and thereby grow and become more profitable. He quickly realized, though, that no amount of fine-tuning and pruning of the portfolio would get the company to the kinds of stretch targets that he had in mind. Welch resorted to edge thinking: Can we achieve unprecedented growth through an acquisitions program of major scope and scale? The answer, in retrospect, was an emphatic yes. But only a leadership team with edge could shape the challenge, and deliver on its potential, the way that GE did.

CHAPTER 4

THE 4E LEADER
EXECUTES

Individuals who have the fourth E get things done. They consistently deliver—in many cases, not just meeting their goals, but blowing them away. They understand that the first three E's are of little value unless they are leveraged to produce results.

For years, there were only three E's at GE. As late as 1998, Welch still wrote of the three "E's." But Welch began to get the sense that something was missing from his formula. Many managers had "energy," "energize," and "edge" in abundance, but they were still coming up short on the numbers. That's when the fourth E was added and the concept of The 4E Leader fully formed. *

Jack Welch succeeded in part because he left so little to chance. In many ways, he was a natural—things came easily to him that confounded many other managers—but he also believed that most leaders are *made*, not born. He wanted to know what the best were made of. Why did some leaders excel, while others only got by?

Welch spent countless hours thinking about this and related questions, and he tried looking through a series of different lenses to

---

*As readers will learn in Chapter 8 it may be open to debate as to *who* came up with the fourth E.

answer his own question. One of these lenses, for example, was a five-question framework. Welch felt that any manager worth his or her salt should be able to provide answers to the following five questions:

1. What does your global competitive environment look like?

2. In the last three years, what have your competitors done?

3. In the same period, what have you done to them?

4. How might they attack you in the future?

5. What are your plans to leapfrog them?

Obviously, managers who could provide compelling answers to these questions had a good grasp on their organization and its competitive environment. But, Welch decided, upon further reflection, even knowing these answers didn't seem to be enough. There were plenty of managers who could answer these questions but who did not execute consistently. Again, Welch zeroed in on his original question: Just what it was that made the best leaders so effective? What did they *do*, and how did they think? What were their leadership "Best Practices" that others could emulate?

To get the answers to these questions, Welch and his HR team (led by Bill Conaty) invited 20 of GE's most promising vice presidents to Fairfield to discuss the topic of leadership. The results gleaned at that meeting ultimately would be shared with thousands of GE managers around the globe.

One of the leadership keys, concluded the group, was to *master the job you have* before focusing on future promotions: "It's great to think about the future, but it's a whole lot better to think about the future when you're hitting the ball out of the park on your current job. Do the job you are on better than anyone has ever done it," said HR Senior Vice President Conaty.

All of the group's conclusions were put into a presentation called "Advice from Successful Executives." The group determined that the leaders who made the greatest contributions were those who excelled in these six areas:

- Performance

- Expertise

- Ownership

- Challenge and visibility

- Mentors/role models

- Global experience/cultural breadth

PERFORMANCE

The key to performing, as suggested earlier, is to excel in the job you have today. Some managers wear their ambition on their sleeves. These were not the types of leaders who tended to prevail in a Welch-run organization. Ambition is a good thing, within reason—even a necessity. But the best way to realize that ambition was not to spend time charting your course up the ladder or playing politics; it was to do your job better than anyone had ever done it. Only after one "hit the ball out of the park" could one begin to think about that next job or promotion.

EXPERTISE

Welch didn't believe in "dabbling." As he saw it, mastering a specific competence or set of skills was critical. Once you had done so, it was incumbent on you to search out ways in which your expertise could be put to use in the larger corporate setting, such as in a cross-functional or a multifunctional team setting. When Welch launched Six Sigma, he made sure that GE developed more experts (master black belts) than any of its rivals. When he asked, hundreds of GE managers responded by learning new skills and taking on new assignments. But they did so only after establishing their expertise in a specific area—functional or otherwise.

OWNERSHIP

In this case, *ownership* implies taking responsibility for one's own fate. It is up to each individual to hone and develop his or her skills. *Hold yourself accountable*, Welch advised, for that is where the responsibility lies. Don't complain about how overworked you are or about how no one appreciates you. Complaining never won anyone a promotion or recognition—or at least, not the type of recognition the complainer might have hoped for. Welch believed strongly that he had to create a learning organization. But he also believed that his people had to be open to learning and had to seek to continuously improve and develop themselves. Welch urged managers to accumulate *knowledge* and *new ideas* rather than titles or promotions.

CHALLENGE AND VISIBILITY

Welch urged managers to "play offense" with their careers. Don't sit back and wait for things to happen; make them happen. Seek out the tough jobs, not the easy assignments. Do the things that really make a difference—the tasks that are most important to the business. This is the best way to gain the kind of visibility and recognition that your ambition leads you to look for.

MENTORS/ROLE MODELS

Because he endorsed the concept of a learning organization, Welch was a big believer in mentors. For example, when he heard that managers in one of his U.K.-based insurance businesses were using younger mentors to teach older managers about the Internet, he loved the idea. Called "reverse mentoring," it became the model that he and his top 1,000 managers used in the United States. Yes, younger people normally learn from older people. But in a time of fast-changing technologies, and in the context of a boundaryless organization, the opposite may very well turn out to be true. Managers have to be prepared to change hats and be students as well as teachers.

GLOBAL EXPERIENCE/CULTURAL BREADTH

Welch implemented his globalization initiative in 1987, before most companies thought to formalize it as an initiative. Welch didn't conceive of GE as a domestic business; he saw the entire world as his marketplace. He asked managers to force themselves out of their comfort zones by seeking out assignments in other countries. He recommended cross-cultural assignments, which afforded individuals the chance to learn—and teach—entirely new competency sets.

One manager who understands execution better than most is Robert Nardelli. As we will examine in Chapter 8, from the minute Nardelli arrived at Home Depot, he never took his eye off the execution ball. He understood that the key to effective execution is being able to juggle all aspects of leadership simultaneously:

I think it's the combination of strategy and people and financial strength that allows us to deliver the consistency and the repetitiveness of our performance year over year. . . . I would encourage other CEOs to lay out a strategy, make sure they're resourcing it, and then bring that strategy to operational reality.

Nardelli also knew the enemy when he encountered it: "We have to continually look outside ourselves. Otherwise you tend to get a level of complacency. Complacency breeds arrogance. Arrogance spirals you down to failure. . . . So we keep pushing ourselves every day. We talk about growth is fundamental to sustainability. If we aren't growing, we're shrinking. There is no status quo in this business. Change is the only constant."

4E LEADERS PLAY OFFENSE WITH THEIR CAREERS

The 4E Leaders understand that there is no substitute for achievement. They develop their expertise and make themselves indispensable to an organization. They master the job they have before thinking about their next promotion. They understand that performance must be achieved today, not a year from now. When given a chance, they take the more challenging assignments, including cross-cultural posts. They know that since nothing is a sure thing, stacking the odds in their favor is the next best thing.

Execution Is a Discipline

As mentioned in Chapter 2, Larry Bossidy, Welch's friend and former vice chairman, and Ram Charan, consultant and author, contributed to the leadership body of knowledge with their national best-seller *Execution*. That work helped to establish execution as a distinct discipline, worthy of study in its own right.

Bossidy and Charan explained that execution is, in itself, a field of study. In essence, it is a set of "behaviors" and competencies that managers need to incorporate into their playbooks. They also describe execution as a critical success ingredient and that absent an execution-oriented culture a firm would have a difficult time maintaining any genuine competitive advantage.

Bossidy and Charan write that many failed corporate strategies failed mainly as a result of poor execution. An organization will execute consistently only if the right culture, practices, rewards, and so on are deeply ingrained in the fabric of the company, and if top management remains involved (execution cannot be delegated). The authors also assert that managers who expend valuable company resources on other programs while ignoring execution are "building houses with no foundations."

Execution is a systematic process of rigorously discussing hows and whats, questioning, tenaciously, following through, and ensuring accountability.

Bossidy and Charan established several other important truths about execution. First, an execution-oriented culture is about getting the dialogue right, and it must be driven from the top down. Leaders can't be afraid to ask the really difficult questions. A culture of execution, however, involves many things—such as setting the right goals, getting the strategy right, candor, rewards, norms, values, and so on—and must be embedded deep into the company. How an organization approaches these vital tasks and systems determines how well it executes.

In order to reward for execution, an organization first needs to measure performance. People need targets—*stretch* goals—in order to be able to quantify their performance and determine whether the division or unit is executing at the desired performance level. A story from Welch's early days at GE makes the point.

Welch spent his first years with GE working in a small plastics business. Looking back in later years, he concluded that this relatively inconsequential operation represented an excellent model for all GE's businesses to emulate: The antithesis of bureaucracy and a bloated organization chart, it was all about speed, excitement, camaraderie, and achievement.

In that plastics lab, the achievement piece was always tied to quantifiable goals. When, for example, he and his team closed a $500 order for plastic pellets, they would celebrate by going out for beers. They also posted the names of every $500 customer on the wall and dubbed it the "$500 club."

They decided that every time they added 10 new names to the $500 club, they would celebrate anew. True, this is a relatively modest example of an achievement-oriented culture in action. But these and similar practices helped Welch create a $26 million plastics business—and helped him become the youngest general manager in GE's history (at age 32).

Nine Steps to Building an Execution Culture

Welch's "$500 club" example illustrates a good technique for building an execution-oriented culture in a small business or

A PORTRAIT IN EXECUTION:
THE FORD MUSTANG

One example of great execution was the creation of the Ford Mustang in the early 1960s. Lee Iacocca (then the newly appointed general manager at Ford, and still years away from his prominent role in saving Chrysler from bankruptcy) was the driving force behind the new car. But for the Mustang to succeed, Iacocca first had to dissuade Henry Ford II ("Hank the Deuce," in the trade) from pursuing a car still in development called the Cardinal.

The company had already sunk $35 million into the Cardinal, but Iacocca was steadfast in his conviction that the Cardinal was a loser and that Ford could ill afford another Edsel-like flop. For any new car to succeed, reasoned Iacocca, it had to appeal to the young, hip market that was taking shape before his eyes. The straight-talking Iacocca finally convinced top management to drop the Cardinal. This was pivotal, as it cleared the way for the Ford Mustang.

Iacocca was certain that the youth market was set to explode. Researchers predicted that the market would double in size by 1970. He knew that unlike the situation facing the ill-fated Edsel, this was "a market in search of a car." To make his vision a reality, he described what the final product would look like. It had to have great styling, strong performance, and a low sticker price. But he went even further by detailing the *character* of the car: "A car that you could drive to the country club on Friday night, to the drag strip on Saturday, and to church on Sunday."

That sounded great, but the company was still smarting over the Edsel debacle and wanted no part in another new-product disaster.

(continued)

Also, managers feared that the new car would cannibalize sales of other Ford automobiles. Iacocca was undeterred: He was convinced that the car market would "be stood on its ear in the next few years." He put together a top-notch team (the "Fairlane Committee") to figure out how to capitalize on this impending seismic shift.

But time was now working against him. He had set the 1964 New York World's Fair as the release date for his new dream model. To beat the clock, he asked his designers to come up with workable designs in only 14 days—a stretch goal by any measure.

The Mustang was a home run from the first day out. When it was released in April 1964, Ford showrooms turned into mob scenes. In one Texas showroom, 15 customers bid on the one Mustang in the window. In its first two years alone, Mustang generated net profits of $1.1 billion (in 1960s dollars)—a staggering success.

The creation of the Mustang is a classic example of how a leader who is rich in the E's can make the right things happen. Iacocca was a tireless manager (*energy*) and was able to convince others to share in his vision of the future (*energize*). In this case, that vision was to abandon one product (the Cardinal) in favor of another (the Mustang). "Maybe" was not in his lexicon (*edge*). He pushed incredibly hard, making his vision a reality. And he succeeded beyond anyone's imagination by delivering eye-popping profits (*execution*).

Although the Mustang was abandoned from time to time (meaning no new models in certain years), it was reintroduced in an entirely new, slickly designed version in 2005, proving one more thing about execution: When you get it just right, its effects may be felt long after that individual leaves the organization.

division. Creating a performance-based culture in a large organization, however—with far-flung and diverse divisions, units, managers, departments, reward systems, and so on—is a much more complex challenge.

It must begin at the top, with the chief executive officer (or division head in the case of a semiautonomous or fully autonomous subsidiary). Of course, much depends on your starting point. As a rule, however, one of the keys to developing an execution culture is the recognition that altering the culture of a Fortune 500 company takes years—there is simply no quick fix or magic potion that can change a company overnight.

The following steps summarize 20 years of deep, difficult cultural change at GE. The Welch record is one of the most complete and well documented of any CEO in history. Each of the following subjects could serve as the focus of a book on its own—and in fact, some have.

1. *Establish performance as a key company priority.* From his first days on the job, Welch made it known that his number 1, number 2 edict would be the new standard of performance at GE. This was followed by his "three circles" and his "fix, close, or sell" imperatives. Collectively, these edicts formed a powerful message: Execution was now the new order of things, and those businesses and individuals that could not help the company win would not be retained.

   Some criticized Welch for being heartless, shortsighted, or insensitive for shedding businesses (and people) that did not measure up. Welch was convinced that any lesser step was unacceptable. There *was* no job security without satisfied customers, and bad companies (or uncommitted employees) can't create satisfied customers. Only healthy, growing businesses can provide jobs, contribute to communities, and foster the personal growth of their employees and managers.

2. *Make sure that the company has a defining set of values.* The hardware decisions and restructuring helped position GE for growth, but it was the shared values that gave the company its soul. Every business is different. The values that best describe your organization should define your organization so that both employees and customers recognize your company in those values. To be worth more than the paper they are written on, they have to be authentic.

   Integrity, boundarylessness, seeing change as an opportunity, being open to ideas from anywhere, killing bureaucracy, being committed to Work-Out and Six Sigma, having global brains—these were the values and priorities that distinguished GE from other companies. The key is to find the things that matter the most at *your* organization and then to spread them around the company like wildfire. Also, put teeth behind those values: Make sure that everyone knows that adhering to the values is the cost of admission.

3. *Organize for execution.* Welch delayered the company early on. He knew that there was far too much muddled complexity, too many managers, too much bureaucracy, and so on. He doubled the average number of managerial direct reports. When he took over, most of GE's managers had about six direct reports, which Welch saw as far too few. That low a ratio only encouraged managers to micromanage. By widening the span of control, he was in effect helping to get the managers off the backs of the organization's rank and file—something that Welch regarded as vitally important to his boundaryless ideal.

Welch also made sure that the ownership of each of the businesses was put back into the hands of the business's leaders, rather than the strategic planners. By delayering, increasing managers' direct reports, and giving businesses back to their leaders, he was structuring an organization that had decentralization as its organizing theme. In retrospect, it was a crucial move. Managing by control from some far-off home office is no way to develop an agile, fast enterprise that has change in its blood.

4. *Use differentiation to promote the A's, keep the B's, and fire the C's.* Welch said that differentiation was one of his most important tools in remaking GE's culture. Every organization must abandon what Welch called "false kindness." False kindness is not telling people the truth. It's keeping an individual on the payroll when you know, deep in your bones, that he or she is not cutting it. The real challenge lies in developing a fair method of evaluating your team—one that separates the A's, the B's, and the C's.

5. *Make execution a key part of the reward system.* Let managers know that bonuses and stock options will be based not on seniority or job ranking but on consistent achievement of vital execution goals. One critical challenge is to make sure to have deep buy-in to the reward system. That is far more difficult in an organization that does not have adequate measures or a performance culture in place. If your firm has gotten away from differentiation and setting strong performance goals, you may need to go back and focus your energies on making sure that steps 1 through 4 are in place before going further.

6. *Use Work-Out or a similar cultural initiative to instill candor and trust into the fabric of the organization.* This is not possible

unless steps 1 through 4 have been implemented first. A company must be committed to performance, must be organized for execution, and must have integrity in its hiring, firing, and promotions. Reward and compensation systems have to be in alignment as well. Trust and openness will not happen by accident, nor will they happen quickly.

Welch could not have launched other key initiatives such as Six Sigma without first creating a performance-based culture in which candor and boundarylessness were the norms. Welch had been in the CEO job for a decade before Work-Out was implemented on a companywide basis. By 1992, more than 200,000 GE employees had been through at least one Work-Out session.

7. *Develop and train your best leaders.* Crotonville became the key to winning the hearts and minds of GE's managers. Before Welch took over, Crotonville was for GE's "second-class citizens." The best managers actually avoided Crotonville— they were "above it." (Remember, Welch himself had attended only one class before he became CEO.) But Welch changed all that. Over time, Crotonville became a place to which only the best and the brightest at GE were invited.

But the most meaningful training in organizations takes place outside the classroom. As a result, the company must foster dialogue and informal meetings every day, all across the organization. Developing new ideas, experimenting with new processes and products—anything that facilitates learning in its most basic forms must be encouraged and nurtured. Finally, there must be a process in place that takes the organization's best ideas and translates them into things that can be acted upon.

8. *Make sure that there is an operating system in place that focuses on execution.* Crotonville was only one part of GE's operating system. In addition, there was an elaborate system of meetings and reviews, including the annual managers' meeting in Boca Raton, the quarterly CEC meetings, Session C, and so on. All of these—as well as the informal meetings and dialogue that took place every day in every GE business—inculcated GE's performance culture deep into the soul of the company.

The GE operating system reinforced all of Welch's company-wide initiatives, such as Globalization and Six Sigma, the company's value system, and so on. Welch would often say or write things like, "Globalization has made 14 trips through the GE operating system." By that he meant that globalization had been a vital part of the meetings and review system for 14 years.

9. *Continue to winnow out weak businesses and weak performers.* In a Welch-like organization, there is no room for under-performers. They will eventually kill the organization. Search out career "dabblers" who have hung on for years without accomplishing anything of note. To really execute, you will need people who exceed expectations on a consistent basis. This is one of the most difficult things to do, but also one of the most necessary.

With his contentious edict of eliminating the bottom 10 percent every year, Welch sent an important message at the same time that he was making his organization stronger: *If you cannot compete at this level, you do not belong here.* That policy became a lightning rod for controversy, but Welch saw it as a necessary step. In sports, the most successful teams keep only the best.

THE NINE STEPS TO AN EXECUTION CULTURE

1. Establish performance as a key company priority.

2. Establish a defining set of values.

3. Organize for execution.

4. Use differentiation as a way to constantly improve the talent base.

5. Make execution a key part of the reward system.

6. Use Work-Out or a similar cultural initiative to instill candor and build trust.

7. Develop, train, and nurture your best leaders.

8. Make sure that there is an operating system in place that focuses on execution.

9. Continue to winnow out weak businesses and weak performers.

Eleven Causes of Poor Execution and How to Deal with Them

Welch sought reasons why people succeeded, but he also wanted to find out why some senior managers *failed* at GE.

Based on the previous pages and chapters, the reader may feel that many of the reasons for failure in Welch's world might be fairly obvious: The unsuccessful leader failed to inspire, did not believe in the company's values, had poor instincts, built walls rather than knocking them down, led by intimidation or fear, and so on.

Here is the list that Welch and his team came up with (paraphrased), as well as some suggestions about what might be done to mitigate each of these failure-inducing factors:

1. *The wrong stuff.* These individuals are what Welch called "bad actors." They did not behave or lead in a manner that was consistent with the company's belief and value system.

    The remedy. Values are a difficult thing to teach. A senior manager who does not believe in the company's values should be eliminated as quickly as possible, lest he or she "infect" colleagues or direct reports.

2. *Poorly conceived organization.* Welch and GE called this the "flawed organization concept." Too many layers, the wrong structure, the wrong expectations, or not giving a unit what it needs to succeed—all of these can derail a manager.

    The remedy: Simplify the organization chart. Work with your senior HR manager to reorganize the company, reducing layers. Consider revamping some parts of the approval system to speed decision making.

3. *Wrong choices.* Organizations sometimes promote the wrong people. No one is perfect, so a manager is bound to make the wrong choice once or twice in his or her career.

    The remedy. Recognizing a bad selection is the first step to fixing this. Once you do, then you either fire that manager or (if appropriate) find him or her another position that he or she is truly suited for. Be careful about the latter approach, though; you may compound your problems by simply sticking that manager somewhere else.

4. *Insufficiently heroic objectives.* This manager is not an effective energizer. He or she has difficulty inspiring others, articulating a vision, and so on.

> *The remedy.* This is a flaw, but it may not be a fatal one. Some managers have a hard time understanding how they are perceived by their peers and their direct reports. Coaching this type of manager with very specific suggestions may help. Also, invite the manager to one or two of your meetings to show him or her how you get others to act.

5. *Poor start.* Some managers get off on the wrong foot and consistently lag behind. This is akin to the runner who doesn't leave the starting block until his rivals are at the 100-meter pole.

> *The remedy.* This is another tough one to overcome. Some managers are simply overwhelmed and never seem to catch up. The first step is to sit down with this manager to sort out the issues. If, after your talk with the manager, you determine that he or she will never do better than tread water, then you have no choice but to fire or reassign him or her. But the same caveats described in the remedy for cause 3 apply.

6. *Cannot adapt.* Having the ability to live with paradox and change is essential skill in a learning organization. Some managers can adapt; other can't. The key is having the ability to fix "fatal flaws."

The remedy: Once again, this is tough to teach. But the only way to address this situation is to attack it head-on. Sit down with the manager and provide very specific feedback on what is *not* getting done. Unless this manager is open to constructive criticism, however, it is unlikely that he or she will be able to turn this around.

7. *Can't get it done.* Some otherwise skilled managers have an extremely difficult time making big decisions. But that's their *job.* Managers have to be equipped to "pull the trigger" when the time comes. They must be able to do more than talk; they must be able to say yes or no (not maybe) when the situation demands it.

The remedy: Some managers fear making a big mistake, whether in hiring, doing a deal, selling or buying a company, or whatever. The best way to correct this is to let the manager know that you, the leader, will not punish him or her for honest mistakes. Tell the manager that it's not necessary to be right 100 percent of the time but to tilt the odds in his or her favor by making the right calculations.

8. *Not in focus.* Managers who are "out of focus" have a hard time discerning the forest from the trees. They lack the ability to transform all the data and information into results that can be acted upon.

The remedy: Once again, this requires coaching. Some managers may need help in figuring out what is important. You need to show them what Welch calls the "leverage points": those things (e.g., decisions and actions) that will really move the needle. Ask them to carefully document leverage points and monitor their progress. This will help them keep their eye on the ball.

9. *Poor instincts.* This is a manager who cannot make the right calls with the limited information that he or she has. These managers seem to have a "tin gut" when it comes to making deals and other important decisions.

   The remedy: The best chance you may have to turn around a manager with bad instincts is to do a postmortem on some of his or her recent misfires. You also may need to monitor this manager's decisions closely so that his or her learning on the job doesn't cost the company dearly.

10. *Ego problems.* Some managers come to believe their own press clippings. They take themselves too seriously, and they don't often take responsibility for their actions. These are people with maturity and value issues.

    The remedy: Like cause 1, this is often a case of a "bad actor." Ego problems are never easy to overcome, and they can cost the organization a great deal. These managers have a way of killing the morale of anyone who runs afoul of them. Do not let a self-important manager destroy your unit or division. Deal with it head-on by removing the offending manager.

11. *Too slow.* "Urgency" is another key Welch watchword. Some managers, often those who lack the first E, energy, seem to move in slow motion.

    The remedy: Once again, coaching is required to help turn these slowpokes around. In a constructive manner, point out what is not getting done quickly enough *and* why moving more quickly is so important to the success of the organization. Work closely with this manger until he or she develops quicker reflexes.

TAKE A PERFORMANCE AUDIT

Take a few minutes to consider the following questions. While this is far from a scientific survey, this informal audit can help you to ascertain how far your organization has to go in developing a performance-based culture.

1. Do people up and down the hierarchy know exactly what constitutes success in your group or division (e.g., revenue, net income, inventory turns)?

2. Are the values (i.e., the "guiding ideas") of your firm clearly stated—and understood by workers up and down the hierarchy?

3. Does your organization enforce the values system by rewarding those who live the values?

4. Does your organization deal with change in a proactive manner?

5. Is the current organizational structure the right one for your industry? That is, does the structure help the organization to execute consistently?

6. Are there fewer than six management layers between the CEO of your company and the hourly paid worker?

7. Do decisions in your organization get made in a timely fashion?

8. Are lines of authority in your group well defined? That is, is it clear who has the ultimate decision-making authority?

9. Do the people who make decisions have access to the data and information they need to make those decisions?

10. Does your organization make use of cross-functional teams?

(continued)

11. Are there good relationships in place between and among managers in different departments (e.g., sales, marketing, and manufacturing)?

12. Are managers aptly rewarded for making and exceeding key performance goals?

13. Are senior managers actively involved in fostering a culture of execution (e.g., do they routinely speak to your group, describe success variables, discuss organizational priorities)?

14. Does your organization employ a differentiation system that rates the best and worst performers?

15. Do the best performers typically get the best raises, promotions, and so on?

16. Are nonperformers weeded out during annual performance reviews?

17. Does your division or group routinely set stretch goals?

18. Does your group celebrate when it makes or exceeds a key performance benchmark or goal?

19. Are learning and training high priorities in your organization?

20. Have you personally been involved in a formal training program within the last six months?

21. Do meetings, annual reviews, and dialogue (informal and formal) get the necessary amount of attention in your organization?

22. Has your organization implemented a mentoring program of any kind in the last year?

23. Do managers in your firm "play offense" with their careers by taking on the most challenging assignments?

24. Does your organization "globalize the intellect" by placing key managers in important international posts?

25. Are the senior managers in your organization rich in The 4E's of Leadership?

Once again, while this is anything but an exact science, it does reveal certain strengths, weaknesses, and tendencies. If you answered yes to the vast majority of the questions, then you work for a very proactive company that probably wins far more than it loses. Conversely, if you answered yes to only a few of the questions, your organization has its work cut out for it.

Here is a more detailed grading system to guide you.

If you answered yes to

20 or more questions: Your organization takes execution seriously and is likely to outperform its competitors consistently and weather downturns far better than its rivals.

15–19: Your organization is doing very well, certainly well above average; however, there may be some room for fine-tuning. Zero in on those areas that require improvement.

10–14: Your organization is in need of some major reengineering. You may have to start at the beginning by reassessing everything, from structure to decision making to the quality of its people.

9 or fewer: Your firm is in dire need of an overhaul. You will most certainly need to do the aforementioned things. In addition, consider bringing in outside consultants to help you and the organization make the tough decisions.

The 4E Leader To-Do List

☐ **Set ambitious performance targets and celebrate when you hit them.** Welch's $500 club is an interesting homespun example. Not only did it establish both an immediate goal (get $500 customers) and a short-term target (get ten $500 customers), but it also made work fun and rewarding. It helped Welch to create a performance-based culture while building a very successful business.

☐ **In order to improve your firm's execution quotient, make a list of the 11 causes of poor execution, and write down the key issues associated with each.** Involve others in the exercise. By dealing with these issues head-on, you will go far in addressing the most relevant behaviors, norms, and so on that determine success in your organization. Once you and your team agree on which areas need improvement, work to tackle these factors one by one. Set specific benchmarks and timetables for each designated issue.

☐ **Train for execution.** Bossidy and Charan explained that companies that do not focus on execution while expending precious resources on other programs will sooner or later find themselves in trouble. In order to make execution a top priority, you will need to build it into the company's playbook in fundamental ways.

☐ **Follow the nine rules for developing a performance culture.** While these rules are intended only as broad strokes, they do provide some guidance as to what goes into creating a genuine culture of execution. The operating system, systematic reviews, training, and dialogue all play an important part.

PART 2

LEADERSHIP LESSONS FROM THE 4E ALL-STARS

If you ask Welch what he considers to be his crowning achievement in his 20-plus years as CEO at GE, he is not likely to mention growth, or profits, or market capitalization. Instead, he will point to the leaders he hired, developed, and nurtured.

No matter where one comes down on the Welch legacy, there is one aspect of his record that is indisputable: *his ability to turn his organization into a leader machine.* Under his direction, GE turned out a greater number of CEOs than any business organization in history. If you asked Welch what he would want written on his tombstone, he would be within his rights to choose the same words that were inscribed on the tombstone of business titan Andrew Carnegie:

Here lies a man

Who knew how to enlist

In his service

Better men than himself

That inscription sums up Welch's philosophy on people and leadership. He has said, pointedly, that he could not make a turbine or an aircraft engine, nor could he direct an episode of *Seinfeld*. On the other hand, he knew how to hire and develop the right people while building an authentic learning organization that was designed to maximize the contributions of all GE employees and managers.

The greatest management thinkers agree that there is nothing more important to a business than the quality of its management. The management team is an organization's costliest resource, asserts Peter Drucker, and the one that "depreciates the fastest and needs the most constant replenishment."

Drucker explained that it takes many years to put together an effective management team, but the same team could be "destroyed in a short period of misrule." He also wrote: "Managers cannot create leaders. It can only create the conditions under which potential leadership qualities become effective; or it can stifle potential leadership."

However he did it, Welch's GE became a management-development institution without peer. The leaders that he trained and nurtured, as well as the future generation of leaders spawned in turn by the Welch disciples, typify The 4E Leader.

It is worth noting that the job of CEO gets more difficult with each passing year. During the five years ending in 2000, something like 40 percent of the leaders of the largest 200 companies in the United States either quit or were forced out of their jobs. In 2003 and 2004, roughly 2 percent of Fortune 1000 CEOs turned over *each month.*

No wonder fewer executives covet the top spot at their companies. In a survey released in late 2004 by public relations firm Burson-Marsteller, 60 percent of the most senior managers at Fortune 1000 companies have no designs on becoming CEO, up from 27 percent in 2001.

That is a remarkable and fundamental change in the psyche of senior managers at large corporations. The reasons are numerous, but one of the chief factors is the risk associated with the job. In light of Sarbanes-Oxley (the corporate-governance legislation that went into effect as a result of the financial scandals of the early 2000s), executives must sign off on every number and decimal point, and they risk fines or stiffer penalties if something does not pass muster.

It is against this tumultuous backdrop that the leaders profiled in the chapters that follow have performed their jobs. During this period—the CEO scandal-riddled era, which was also a period of weak global economic performance—being a chief executive was never more difficult. Yet these men performed with distinction.

It seems only appropriate, therefore, in the second half of this book to highlight a handful of these Welch protégés and describe briefly the tactics and lessons they implemented in their new positions. Their own accomplishments, and those of the leaders that they themselves developed, are likely to stand as Welch's greatest legacy.

Welch certainly understands this, and he rarely misses an opportunity to talk up his protégés. For example, when discussing the three men who were in contention for his job (Jeff Immelt, Jim McNerney, and Bob Nardelli), he described them as "sensational" and their performance as "off the charts." All three "exceeded every expectation that we set for them," declared the former GE chairman.

Of the leaders that follow, all but one are "first-generation" Welch protégés, meaning that they reported directly to Welch for several years. But to illustrate the pervasive influence of a 4E Leader like Welch, I have included one "second-generation" Welch leader—that is, one executive who did not report directly to Welch but who instead worked for his successor. Vivek Paul, CEO of India's up-and-coming Wipro, reported to Jeff Immelt during Immelt's final years as head of GE Medical Systems.

What follows, then, are the leadership lessons of five managers who were schooled in the Welch way.

CHAPTER 5

"BLOW IT UP"

How Jeff Immelt Reinvented the House that Jack Built

Companies that seek to compete and grow will need to rely more and more on technology and ideas to innovate. . . . Without innovation, you can't survive. Without it, GE won't see the next 100 years.

—JEFF IMMELT, Chairman and CEO, GE

J eff Immelt was one of three candidates in contention for the most coveted job in corporate America: CEO and chairman of GE.

Although Jack Welch was not scheduled to step down until 2001, he started working on the process of identifying his successor several years earlier. That is standard operating procedure at GE, a company that has led the way in succession planning for a century.

One of the key factors behind Immelt's selection was his devotion to Six Sigma, the quality program that consumed Welch in his last years on the job. But Immelt's relative youth also was important to Welch. Welch wanted to make sure that his successor had enough time to reinvent the company, much as he (and his six predecessors) had done. And there was another advantage to longevity in the CEO's post, as Welch saw it.

As he explained later, Welch's goal in selecting a successor was to choose someone who had enough time to stay in the post for about two decades. Welch had 20 years as CEO, and he wanted to make sure that the person who followed him had as much time as he did to reinvent the company. Also, a longer time frame would help keep that person's feet planted firmly on the ground knowing that he would have to live with any decison— and any blunder—for a very long time.

Flawless Execution . . . Well, Nearly

Of course, one of the other driving forces behind Welch's decision to promote Immelt was Immelt's ability to execute consistently. He had spent many years as head of GE Plastics before taking over as head of GE Medical Systems. In three years there, he nearly doubled revenues, from $3.9 billion to $7.2 billion in 2000. He also strengthened GE's competitive position in Europe and made GE Medical number 1 in its market in Asia.

He also created a business archetype that became a model for other GE businesses. In *Jack*, Welch described it as follows: "Jeff had taken our medical systems business to new levels. He came up with the concept of a global product company that will be a model for almost every business in the company, sourcing intellect, components, and finished products from every corner of the world."

At the same time, Immelt had faced his fair share of problems. As head of GE Plastics, he had made some bad calls and had missed his 1994 net income target by some $50 million (he grew earnings by 7 percent against a budget of 20 percent). Immelt, ill accustomed to missing budgets, was at a loss for how to best handle Welch in this situation.

Upon arriving in Boca Raton for the annual managers' meeting, he avoided Welch like the plague. When Welch finally caught up with him, Welch told him that he loved him, but that if he didn't turn things around, he would fire him. Immelt told Welch he wouldn't have to; if he couldn't do better, he would take himself out.

As it turned out, neither had anything to worry about. Immelt hit the ball out of the park in his final years before being named CEO. His execution earned him ever-increasing bonuses (ballooning by 40 to 50 percent each year), as well as Welch's laudatory handwritten notes (full of exclamations like "wow"). Both the GE board and Welch were convinced that Immelt was the right man at the right time to lead GE.

After telling him that he would get the job, Welch sent one of his signature handwritten notes: "Congratulations on everything— your year at Medical, your selection as CEO of the best company in the world. I know you were really good—but you are even better than I could imagine."

THE 4E LEADER RISES AFTER HE FALLS

Immelt still remembers that fateful day when Welch almost fired him for his awful performance in 1994 (he wrote about it in his 2003 GE Letter to Stakeholders). Rather than lick his wounds, Immelt doubled his efforts to make the business better—and succeeded. The lesson is that anyone can have a bad year; it's what you *do* about it that counts.

Reinvent the Company—Again

As Jack Welch's hand-picked successor, no one had bigger shoes to fill than Jeff Immelt.

Many thought that Immelt would fall on his face. A whole new species of business pundits—the Immelt critics—materialized almost overnight. To be fair, this was less a case of Immelt being perceived as incompetent and more a case of his having the bad luck to succeed a bigger-than-life corporate folk hero. Anyone who followed Jack Welch was likely to suffer by comparison.

And Immelt's honeymoon period was unmercifully short—almost nonexistent. He had the bad luck of being at the helm when GE's decade-long double-digit earnings gains came to an end in 2002. But the "reversal" was inevitable, regardless of who was in possession of the corner office. Growing a $130 billion business by double digits is a lot harder than growing a $25 billion business (the size of GE when Welch took over), and the global economic recession helped to ensure the snapping of the string.

Breaking with the past is a time-honored tradition of incoming CEOs at GE. Reg Jones, Welch's predecessor, gave Welch the same advice that Welch passed on to Immelt: "*Blow it up.*" In other words, tear up the old game plan and create a new one tailored to whatever new realities the company was confronting.

At first, Immelt seemed to shun the advice. Instead, he seemed to be reading off the established Welch script. For instance, in a single week in the fall of 2003, he acquired two huge properties: Vivendi Universal and British medical imager Amersham (with price tags of $14 billion and $10 billion, respectively).

Those two acquisitions were the largest in GE's history (although the $45 billion Honeywell acquisition would have been far larger had Welch been allowed to complete the deal). Immelt, showing signs of Welch-like *edge*, plunged ahead with both these deals, evidently feeling confident that both acquisitions would grow faster than the economy.

But the notion that Immelt was simply imitating Welch was short-lived. A month after acquiring Vivendi Universal and Amersham, Immelt decided to break off parts of the slower-growing insurance companies and combine them in a new entity called Genworth. In a direct repudiation of Welch's strategy, Immelt proclaimed that "insurance [was] simply not the right business for us in the future." That one decision freed up some $4.5 billion in cash.

Welch's acquisitions, as noted previously, accounted for about 40 percent of GE's growth during his tenure. Immelt's early acquisitions (which included the cable channels Telemundo and Bravo) actually *slowed* growth in the short term, but strengthened the company's long-term business outlook. This may seem counterintuitive, but *Fortune's* Jerry Useem understood what Immelt was trying to do: "Immelt isn't buying growth so much as the ability to grow."

Welch's greatest growth machine was GE Capital and GE's rich financial services portfolio; Immelt is exiting some of those businesses and markets. Welch believed in developing GE's leaders by moving them quickly from promotion to promotion, creating a company of talented *generalists*. Immelt's revolving door spins more slowly, ensuring a rich crop of *specialists*.

And Immelt also has put his own stamp on the company's relationship with Wall Street. Welch held sway over analysts by setting lofty quarterly goals and beating them like clockwork. Immelt is taking the long view: outlining a long-term vision and deemphasizing the short term.

In fact, Immelt's entire approach is one that favors the next quarter century over the next fiscal quarter. Unlike many large-company CEOs, Immelt knows that—barring some unanticipated event—his job is safe for 20 years. Few American CEOs have that luxury.

The real paradoxical twist is that by breaking with GE's past, Immelt is in fact being *faithful* to it. Most of GE's chairmen have carved their own paths, and this potentially risky penchant for reinventing the company every couple of decades or so has reaped great rewards for the company.

"Instead of announcing some half-baked turnaround scheme," *Fortune*'s Useem wrote, "he can actually do the things leaders are supposed to do. Develop an intelligent plan. Shore up the finances. Inspire the troops. Invest in the customers. Refrain from making dumb promises."

THE 4E LEADER BALANCES SHORT TERM AND LONG TERM

Given the intense short-term demands on most managers, it is easy to be obsessed with day-to-day sales, decisions, and problems. The 4E Leader understands the importance of making responsible decisions that help the organization both short term and long term.

Blow Up the Business Portfolio

One of the best ways to gain insight into how GE's CEOs "blow up the business" is to examine how each has reshuffled the business portfolio. The way the CEO attacks this task reveals a good deal about his vision of the organization. Under Welch, for instance, there was his signature "three-circles strategy," which defined the future of GE as being in three areas:

Core (GE Lighting)

Technology (medical devices, aircraft engines)

Services (GE Capital)

Like most good strategies, this one was rooted in simplicity. When the three circles were combined with Welch's number 1, number 2 edict and his "fix, close, or sell" imperative, it provided a three-dimensional picture of what GE was, what it wasn't, and what it would become.

A strategy that can answer all three of those questions is rare indeed.

In the beginning of 2004, Immelt set his sights on reshuffling the business portfolio yet again, consolidating GE's portfolio of 13 businesses into 11 that were "focused on markets and customers." Immelt does not see the world in circles. Instead, he set out to define GE's businesses not by its products and offerings, as Welch had done, but by each business's *growth potential,* as outlined as follows:

"Growth engines" were just that—businesses that had the best prospects for double-digit growth (e.g., NBC, Commercial

Finance). In recent years, these businesses had grown by 20 percent per year and contributed 85 percent of GE's earnings. Most of these businesses are leaders in their respective markets, global businesses that leverage GE's great technology base into some sustainable competitive advantage.

"Cash generators" consisted of GE's more cyclical businesses with strong cash flows. The cash generators (e.g., Advanced Materials and Insurance) bring in about 15 percent of the company's earnings. Immelt is quick to point out that although these businesses do not grow as quickly as the growth engines, they do have the potential to grow at a double-digit rate in a strong economy.

In December 2003, in GE's annual business outlook, Immelt proclaimed: "85 percent of the company is in businesses that are to die for," meaning global businesses with a sustainable competitive advantage, double-digit earnings growth, technology leadership, strong service revenues, or a top financial business. He also predicted that 9 of GE's 11 businesses would grow at

FOCUS ON GROWTH ENGINES

Focus on the growth engines by making strategic acquisitions that can strengthen the portfolio. Devote the majority of the company's best resources (people and capital) to these companies and/or divisions, and you should see the payoff within two to three years. Had Immelt not reorganized, there is a high probability that the company would have grown by 9 percent in 2005, not the 14 percent it now predicts.

double-digit rates in the years ahead. (In 2004 GE grew revenues by 14 percent to $152.4 billion)

Initiatives Define the Agenda

There are other significant differences in the way Immelt defined GE. Welch's values (e.g., "be open to change," "boundaryless-ness") and companywide initiatives (e.g., Six Sigma) dominated his agenda. He referred to them often—in GE's annual reports, in speeches to shareowners, and in media interviews. Welch was passionate about these initiatives, and his rhetoric confirmed it:

We have change in our blood.

You have to be on the lunatic fringe when it comes to Six Sigma.

Digitization is changing the DNA of the company every day.

WELCH'S FOUR INITIATIVES

Globalization: The first growth initiative, launched in 1987.

Product Services: Launched in 1995, it came to define the new GE.

Six Sigma: The statistically based quality initiative, launched in 1996, consumed Welch in his final years as CEO and saved the company billions.

Digitization (the "e-initiative"): Although GE was late to the Internet (2000), Welch made up for that by turning GE into a very effective online company (e.g., sales and suppliers).

Clearly, Welch believed fervently in GE and its people, and that passion came through in his speeches and writings. Immelt appears to be just as committed, but his rhetoric is not as flamboyant as Welch's. He also comes at the initiatives from a somewhat different perspective from Welch's. He puts all his initiatives under the banner of "GE's Growth Strategies," aimed at creating "high-margin, capital-efficient growth."

Although Immelt did not abandon the best of what Welch contributed, he "blew it up" by charting a new growth agenda and altering the business portfolio. Immelt is quietly performing a transformation of GE in a very short time:

> *Two important lessons were reinforced for me last year:*
> *the value of context, and the importance of driving change.*
> *By "context," I mean understanding the important global trends*
> *and their impact on GE. I believe we are going through a time*
> *of rapid and meaningful changes to the economic environment.*
> *My belief has only increased my desire to accelerate change*
> *at GE. GE must look different . . . act different . . .*
> *be different . . . to excel in the years ahead.*

Don't Throw the Baby Out . . .

In reinventing the company, Immelt knew that GE already did some things incredibly well. The key was to build on the company's strengths while making the necessary changes. That certainly was true of Six Sigma, the quality initiative launched by Welch and wholeheartedly adopted by his successor. Immelt has a master's degree in applied statistics and is an ardent fan of the quality program that turned Welch—in his own words—into a "fanatic."

Declares Immelt, "There is not one person in GE who is not going to know how to do this."

In 2002, GE completed a staggering 10,000 customer-driven special projects. The company says that 40 percent of its customers want to participate in this form of knowledge- and productivity-boosting program. GE offers its customers a hard-to-turn-down menu of initiatives:

- *Six Sigma knowledge sharing.* Welch made Six Sigma the gospel at GE in the late 1990s. Immelt took this one step further by offering its intricate Six Sigma knowledge to its customers.

- *GE's signature cultural initiatives.* All of the trademark Welch initiatives, from Work-Out to boundarylessness to developing an operating system that fosters learning, are now available to GE's customers as part of this program.

- *Research, facts, and figures.* A $150-plus billion powerhouse generates tons of market research, data, and so on. The company now shares much of this vital information with its customers.

- *GE, a global engine.* GE's first companywide initiative was globalization, which Welch initiated in 1987. The evolution of GE's globalization initiative was a textbook case on how to do it. "Globalizing the intellect" had become a mantra at GE by the time Welch retired. Under Immelt, GE is showing its customers how to duplicate GE's great success in this arena.

Five New Realities

In 2004, Immelt changed the game, just as Welch did in the early 1980s. He reorganized the company around markets "to simplify our operations and deepen our relationship with customers."

Immelt learned long ago that one of the keys to building a growth company is to understand the realities of the global marketplace and make the necessary strategic adjustments (he learned the "face reality" rule from Welch). For example, Immelt points out that the environment for growth in 2004 is not as strong as it had been in the prior few years. To grow, the company must be agile enough to deal with these realities:

1. *A more "interdependent global economy,"* marked by a capacity glut that has spurred pricing battles. This is what has kept unemployment up and margins down.

   Immelt's solution: The key, insists the GE chairman, is to commit resources to innovation and devise new business models/revenue opportunities from current businesses.

2. *A new economic era in which low-cost manufacturers from countries like India and China* are bringing about a new paradigm, as technically skilled workers (e.g., engineers) in these countries are paid only a fraction of what their U.S counterparts receive.

   Immelt's solution: "Winning companies must think globally, but understand local consequences." This solution also has its roots in Welch's "globalize the intellect" imperative. GE has developed a successful strategy of selecting local managers to run its global businesses.

3. *Next is the "consolidation of distribution channels."* This actually helps customers, but at the same time it exerts even more pressures on profit margins.

   Immelt's solution: To win, organizations like GE must have *direct* relationships with customers (e.g., direct sales forces), keep costs in check, and offer a unique customer proposition and value that link GE's profitability to that of its customers.

4. *The potential for new growth platforms in the face of "unstoppable demographics."* Going forward, Immelt is looking for long-term, sustainable growth in fast-growing markets in which his firm has some competitive advantage (e.g., a technological base).

Immelt's solution: Focus on high-growth markets in which GE can leverage its strengths to achieve a sustainable competitive advantage.

5. *An unsure world.* Immelt understands that terrorism, stock market crashes, and other financial and geopolitical events can change the world overnight.

Immelt's solution: The key to success in the future will come from preserving the faith of customers, investors, and employees. The key to maintaining that confidence is through "financial and cultural strength."

While making some important and deep changes, Immelt has been careful not to throw the baby out with the bathwater. Perhaps most importantly, he has retained—and built upon—several of the strong foundations that Welch established during his run. Values, initiatives, the operating system: All were deeply entrenched in the foundation of the company when Immelt took over.

He also added an important new concept, called "At the Customer, For the Customer" (ACFC). This took Welch's concept of customer focus to a new level by institutionalizing the importance of the customer in a way that could be acted upon. "At the Customer" is literally that: being with customers or establishing an office in close proximity to the customer.

"For the Customer" means putting yourself in the customer's shoes: learning the customer's priorities, processes, business,

IDENTIFY THE NEW REALITIES OF YOUR MARKETS AND BE FLEXIBLE ENOUGH TO MAKE THE NECESSARY ADJUSTMENTS

Markets do not stand still. Hundreds of factors exert influence on your firm and the markets in which it operates. Don't get complacent. Once you have identified the key game-changing trends, work with your team to make the necessary shifts in strategy. Be careful to retain the best parts of your company and its processes while making changes to improve challenged businesses, product lines, and other elements.

industry, and so on. The idea is to make it your job to help your customer succeed: His or her worries are your worries. The customer's success is your success. It is apparent that this kind of partnering will become more commonplace at GE and other forward-looking organizations in the years ahead as more educated customers come to expect this quality of service from "partners" like GE.

The Five-Initiative Growth Strategy

Like almost any truly effective CEO, Immelt is obsessed with growing the company. His stated goal is to make sure that the organic growth of GE comes in at 8 percent (excluding acquisitions) while simultaneously keeping the company's high margins. His mantra is

Growth is the initiative, the core competency
we are building at GE.

He points to the company's five-initiative strategy as the key to creating "high-margin, capital-efficient growth":

- Technical leadership

- Services

- Customer focus

- Globalization

- Growth platforms

Technical leadership. Immelt puts technical expertise at the top of his list. He says that this kind of technical leadership, combined with GE's innovative spirit, infuses the company's key initiatives. The company has thousands of researchers in GE's Global Research Centers around the globe, and this group has helped GE stay on top in many markets, ranging from aircraft engines to energy-saving gas turbines.

Welch, too, understood the importance of technical leadership. This explains why he exited from those businesses or markets in which technical leadership provided no competitive advantage—for example, GE Housewares, a company that by the early-to-mid 1980s had become little more than a middleman for Asian knock-offs.

Services. Welch saw services as a critical growth engine, and Immelt certainly has picked up where Welch left off. Immelt also points out that GE has an incredible base of industrial products—including jet engines, power turbines, and medical devices—upon which future service lines may well be built.

Immelt believes that the key to growing this segment in the future is ensuring that GE's service businesses make GE's *customers more profitable.*

Customer focus. Immelt has taken the concept of customer focus to the next level. He created a sales and marketing "council" designed to introduce Six Sigma to GE's customers, thereby improving the alignment of GE's sales force with its customers' needs. One of the home runs in this area is what Immelt calls "vertical selling, the practice of aligning our offerings in four industries that are critical to GE: healthcare, energy, transportation, and retail." These businesses are responsible for close to $50 billion in revenues and roughly $170 billion in financial services assets.

Globalization. Welch's first initiative was globalization. It is now a "core competency" of the company. Global revenues have been growing by double digits for years, and about one-third of GE's leaders are outside the United States. Immelt understands that global success depends on an organization's ability to grow its businesses through relationships and on hiring and developing local managers who grasp the subtle cultural nuances that are so critical to success.

Growth platforms. One of GE's key strengths, writes Immelt, is having the vision to see "unstoppable trends." For example, he predicts that in the near term, the organic growth rate of industrial platforms will be in double digits (in fact, it was 14 percent in 2003). Immelt also asserts that GE has made growth almost second nature, thanks to a regimented approach: "First, we segment broad markets and launch with a small platform acquisition. Then we transform the business model using our growth initiatives, such as services and globalization. Finally, we apply our financial strength to invest in organic growth or acquisitions."

Align Values with Spirit

Shared values have guided the behavior of GE employees and managers since the mid-1980s. As discussed previously, Welch used the GE values to differentiate GE from other companies and, even more important, to explain to all who worked for GE what behaviors the company expected:

Have a Passion for Excellence and Hate Bureaucracy

Have the Self-Confidence to Involve Everyone and Behave in a Boundaryless Fashion.

In a recent executive training session, GE's senior leaders suggested that the company alter its values in order to help tell the story of GE as a growth company. Immelt explained that values cannot simply be rhetoric. If they are really going to shape future behavior, they must be able to be acted upon. And they also must be simple, apply to all, and be motivational.

Remarkably, Immelt and his team condensed GE's shared values into four words:

Imagine

Solve

Build

Lead

While these four words appear to be a pretty significant departure from Welch's more descriptive values, they share many of the same sentiments. And it is worth noting that Welch paved the way for these "values in shorthand" by instilling a solid foundation into the hearts and minds of GE managers and employees.

Imagine. The liberty to aspire and the ability to turn dreams into reality. In order to imagine, one must have the values of passion and curiosity. This value captures the essence of Welch's learning organization, as well as his love of new ideas.

Solve. This speaks to GE's technical leadership and its ability to take on the world's most difficult problems. *Solve* requires resourcefulness and accountability, as well as a solutions mind-set.

Build. This means a great deal at GE. To build necessitates a performance-based culture that creates value for customers and shareholders alike. *Build* also refers to GE's values of teamwork and commitment.

Lead. Welch always preferred the term *leader* to *manager*. *Lead* here means all the things that Welch—and now Immelt—instilled into the soul of the company: openness, optimism, confidence, energy. To lead, one must not only accept change but also view it as an opportunity. To lead is to mount victory upon victory in the marketplace.

In Chapter 1 of this book, Peter Senge's ideas on creating an authentic learning culture were presented in a three-tiered model. The first item in his model explained that "without guiding ideas, there is no passion, no overarching sense of direction or purpose."

That's what values need to accomplish. Whether you work for a small business or a large company, it is the values of the organization that help to guide behavior, give purpose and direction, and provide some feeling of mission. Whether it is done in four words or four paragraphs, the key is to use values to help the people in your organization understand what makes your organization unique—what makes it tick.

Finally, the values of the organization should be consistent. Even if they are revised from time to time—as they have been at GE over the last 20 years—they should not change so drastically that they send mixed signals to the troops. Immelt changed the values, as well the company tagline (from "We Bring Good Things to Life" to "Imagination at Work"), but he didn't alter the bedrock beliefs that made GE a great company.

The 4E Leader To-Do List

☐ **Become growth-obsessed.** Immelt says that growth is the imperative—it is the core competency of GE. Insert that kind of singleness of purpose into your organization. Make growth the focal point of the company's efforts. Energize by creating a vision of growth, and help make that a reality by working with key leaders and employees in your group. However it is stated, the message should always be clear, at every level of the organization: *We must all contribute to the growth of the enterprise.*

☐ **Balance short term with long term.** The acquisitions that Immelt made may have slowed GE's growth in the short term, but they positioned the company for long-term growth. Don't make key decisions without thinking through the ramifications for both the short term and the long term.

☐ **Don't be afraid to blow up the business portfolio.** Stay abreast of all key trends and forces affecting your business, its customers, and the industry as a whole. Every so often it would be useful for you to take a good look at each of your businesses and product lines. Do not be afraid to exit from markets that you would not enter and enter new markets if your chance of success looks strong.

CHAPTER 6

MAKE LEADERSHIP DEVELOPMENT A TOP PRIORITY

How James McNerney Built on the Welch Playbook

*Leadership development is about helping people grow,
and if I can get people as individuals growing, then
I've got a company that grows.*

—JAMES McNERNEY, Chairman of the Board and CEO, 3M

In 2000, James McNerney was one of the other two executives who did not get Welch's job.

After McNerney found out that he had lost out to Jeff Immelt, he told Welch, flat out, that Welch had picked the wrong guy. But McNerney didn't waste time worrying about his lost opportunities at GE. He landed on his feet and then some, becoming chairman and CEO of corporate juggernaut 3M, the first outsider to head up that company in its 100-plus-year history.

Investors applauded 3M's decision to bring in McNerney. In the five years prior to his arrival, 3M's stock had lagged behind both the Dow and the S&P 500. The day that word of McNerney's appointment to his new post hit the street, 3M's market value skyrocketed by some $4.5 billion. Since then, McNerney has been widely lauded as the most successful CEO of the "GE graduate class" of 2001 (the year Welch left and Immelt took over) and one of the most effective business leaders of his day.

Before arriving at GE, McNerney had paid his dues at Procter & Gamble and consulting-industry heavyweight McKinsey & Company. His record at GE was impeccable, and (except for that last elusive rung) his ascent up the company ladder was fast and sure. Along the way, he served as CEO of GE Lighting and Asia Pacific Operations and, in his last three years, as CEO of GE Aircraft Engines. During that final three-year stint, the aircraft engines business grew by more than 20 percent per year and delivered more profit than any other GE unit.

In 2004, *BusinessWeek* named McNerney one of the world's best managers. Since 2001, when he announced a major five-part productivity program (see sidebar), 3M's stock is up more than 50 percent (versus a single-digit decrease in the S&P 500). While McNerney is popularly known as a "quant jock," he is also a leader who embodies the 4E model. He has an abundance of energy, sparks others to perform, and has executed consistently throughout his career.

He also knows how to make the daunting decisions. 3M, which started as a sandpaper manufacturer in 1902, had fallen on relatively hard times by the end of the twentieth century. In 2001, McNerney's first full year at 3M, he eliminated 6,000 jobs and closed the doors on seven plants. He followed that up in 2002 with additional layoffs and plant closings.

Like the earlier layoffs at GE, these cost-cutting moves were controversial. Certainly some people at 3M agreed that McNerney had to take these hard steps, but there were also many at the company who had a difficult time facing new realities. McNerney was undaunted: "I've got to make it culturally okay to say no," explained the 3M chairman in mid-2002. Saying no and sticking to your guns are habits of leaders with edge.

At the same time, McNerney established a profile as the kind of leader who was prepared to provide the vision and get out of the way (i.e., strong energizer), letting his people determine the specific

MCNERNEY'S FIVE-PART PRODUCTIVITY PLAN

1. *Drive Six Sigma* throughout the company so that it becomes the common language for all of 3M's businesses.

2. *"Global sourcing,"* that is, using 3M's global scope and centralized purchasing function to find the best prices and reduce the overall number of suppliers.

3. *"Indirect cost reduction"* via tighter measures and controls (e.g., on T&E).

4. *"E-productivity,"* a program similar to GE's digitization initiative that means better management of the company's Web investments.

5. *"3M Acceleration,"* a program to leverage the firm's research and development (R&D) and increase the company's speed to market.

(source: *Industry Week*)

145

path for getting to the target. He was determined, he made it clear, to drive change from the bottom up.

Don't Undervalue Leadership

One of the keys to McNerney's success was his willingness to rip up the strategic plan that was in place at 3M when he took over. Global markets were then deep in their early-twenty-first-century swoon, making the business plan that he inherited "irrelevant" (in his assessment). From day one, in other words, he found himself living one aspect of the Welch doctrine: rewriting his agenda on a moment's notice.

Actually, the circumstances of McNerney's arrival at 3M in 2000 bore more than a few resemblances to Welch's own arrival at GE decades earlier. First and foremost, McNerney faced tough economic conditions, which ensured that he would have an uphill battle on his hands from the outset. Instead of using that as an excuse, however, he raised the bar by setting ambitious objectives. He established a growth goal of 10 percent—roughly *double* 3M's growth rate during the preceding decade:

> *In the old world—the '70s, '80s, and '90s—you could get away with either running the place very productively . . . or growing [the business]. . . . In today's world, our overall business objectives are to be simultaneously strong in operating excellence and unusually strong in organic growth.*

The results since the establishment of these kinds of stretch goals have been truly impressive. In 2003, McNerney's 3M achieved record year-over-year earnings for the seventh quarter in a row— a lofty performance that has won the hearts of employees and shareholders alike.

McNerney also has earned a platinum reputation among the CEO elite. Gerard R. Roche, senior chairman at the recruitment firm of Heidrick & Struggles International, told *Fortune* that "people come to us and say, 'Go get us a Jim McNerney.'" *Fortune* writes that McNerney's name routinely comes up when a Fortune 100 company is in need of a leader, from Coke to Disney to Merck. His management style is one part carrot, one part stick:

> *Some people think you either have a demanding, command-and-control style or you have a nurturing, encouraging style. . . . I believe you can't have one without the other.*

His new agenda at 3M includes tighter fiscal management, more ambitious budget goals, and a greater emphasis on leadership development. Like Jack Welch, Jim McNerney leads by example. He is intimately involved in the company's executive training program, declaring it "fundamental" for a CEO to take a leading role in the company's human-development efforts.

McNerney has established leadership development as one of the company's priorities. He turned 3M's R&D training center in St. Paul into the company's version of GE's Crotonville. Called the Leadership Development Institute, it trains some 40 "high-potential people" at a time in a 17-day "Accelerated Leadership Development Program."

The entire program is devoted to solving company problems personally identified and selected by CEO McNerney. On the final day of the course, McNerney listens to the class's solutions, some of which subsequently have been implemented companywide. Like GE's Crotonville, it is also a place that educates managers in key company initiatives like Six Sigma:

*My experience is that if people are convinced they're growing
as they pursue company goals, that's when you get ignition.*

The fact that 3M had a long-established culture of collegiality
actually made McNerney's task more difficult. The problem was
that "collegiality" drifted all too easily into being undisciplined and
undemanding. McNerney came from a battle-hardened company
with a finely honed performance culture; he now headed a company that had not been forced to face reality. He knew that changing the company meant imposing more discipline and placing a
greater focus on execution and performance.

For example, he insisted that all 3M employees get graded on the
same kind of vitality curve used at GE. Before McNerney's arrival,
the 3M compensation system was equally generous to high performers and relative laggards. For example, any manager above a
certain grade level received stock options regardless of his or her
performance. The system rewarded seniority for seniority's sake,
without much linkage to *achievement*. McNerney quickly changed
that policy, insisting that only those managers with strong performance metrics should be granted options. Says McNerney:

*3M had a tendency to overvalue experience
and undervalue leadership.*

He also sharpened the company's focus on growth. Before he
arrived, all units were assigned the same budget target regardless
of the unit's performance or potential. McNerney's approach was
far more strategic.

Just as Jeff Immelt emphasized GE's growth engines, McNerney
focused on the 3M businesses with the greatest prospects for
growth. He apportioned research and marketing dollars based on
each business's perceived growth potential. That meant, for example,

GROW PEOPLE TO GROW THE BUSINESS

Every large company needs its own Crotonville or something like it. "Leadership development is about helping people grow, and if I can get individuals growing, then I've got a company that grows," says McNerney. The key is having a place in which the next generation of leaders can learn the language—and initiatives—that will guide the company in the years ahead.

more resources for health care—3M's largest business, with more than $4 billion in sales and $1 billion in operating revenues.

McNerney knows that the key to the future lies in improving the way his company *executes*. He understands what the company can control and what the company can't:

> *We know we can't manage the global economy . . . but we can manage ourselves, our new product introductions, and our costs. And in that way shape our success.*

Adapting the Welch Playbook

In addition to leadership development and a more strategic approach to managing the business portfolio, McNerney also implemented several other GE initiatives at 3M. These included Welch's signature strategy, Six Sigma.

In fact, McNerney embraced this statistically driven quality program with the same fanaticism as Welch, convinced that it could prove to be one of the real keys to success at 3M. Again, there was some resistance, but McNerney discounted the idea that the rigorous program would have any adverse effect on the company's culture:

The same energy and entrepreneurism is being funneled
and structured. I don't think we want to lose that.
We just want to discipline that.

What was behind this statement? When McNerney arrived at 3M, he discovered that the company had a "menu approach" to quality and process improvement. In other words, Six Sigma was one of several quality-oriented programs that managers could choose among. He ended that practice, making Six Sigma 3M's sole quality program. He knew how important it was for the entire company to "develop a common language" while also "leveraging [the company's] size."

McNerney takes great pride in the results his company has achieved with Six Sigma, which he says 3M adopted with record speed. The initiative began with the manufacturing organization, then moved into the backroom, finance, HR, and customer-service operations. But McNerney didn't stop there. One lesson he had learned at GE was the importance of making sure that the customers "feel" the effects of Six Sigma. The company is now focused on partnering with customers and assisting them to enhance their own business processes. Six Sigma means

Being more responsive to customers, driving processes that
are more efficiently implemented. Six Sigma is a perfect
way to go about this. . . . We're using the same language,
focusing on the same metrics, sharing the same successes.

During a three-day summit with quality guru Dr. Joseph Juran in June 2002, McNerney made a compelling presentation that

USE SIX SIGMA TO ALIGN THE IMPROVEMENT EFFORT WITH BUSINESS STRATEGY AND CULTURAL TRANSFORMATION

McNerney told Dr. Juran that in addition to the tangible benefits of Six Sigma (e.g., lower costs, increased ROI), Six Sigma also can improve the company's capabilities and transform the organization "toward a more fact-based culture." McNerney understands that any improvement strategy, especially one as ambitious as Six Sigma, must be aligned with the business strategy and any "long-term transformation" of the company.

explained how 3M would use the quality initiative to "drive financial performance, growth and leadership development." He added that in the process, Six Sigma also would help to transform a corporate culture that over the years had bred complacency. McNerney reported that as a result of Six Sigma, the company had grown its revenues, reduced expenses, and increased both productivity and cash flow.

Like Welch, McNerney never misses a chance to talk up the benefits of Six Sigma. Since Six Sigma is being used for everything from sales techniques to new-product development, a greater percentage of managers are being trained in it each year.

As of the spring of 2004, about 25 percent of the 3M employees who had been trained in Six Sigma had been promoted at least twice. And because of the program's quantitative approach and measurements, it presents the added benefit of helping to identify the next generation of 3M leaders.

"Globalize the Intellect"

Six Sigma is not the only "Welch trademark" program that McNerney adapted successfully at 3M. In the international arena, 3M (which has operations in more than 60 countries and does business in more than 120) has made progress in "globalizing the intellect" of the company. And 3M uses local managers to run its international businesses, a strategy that was pivotal to GE's successful globalization initiative.

In his time at 3M, McNerney has invested far more heavily in markets outside the United States, especially those with the best growth potential. While reducing headcount and capital budgets in the United States, he has increased capital budgets and ramped up hiring in some of the fastest-growing markets in Asia. This is consistent with McNerney's ambitious double-digit growth plan. Here he sums up his approach to globalization while addressing the controversial issue of outsourcing:

> *I'm responsible for keeping 3M a globally competitive company.*
> *Now it's very hard to serve Chinese customers in a lot of our*
> *businesses unless we're manufacturing there. We don't do*
> *this to eviscerate U.S. jobs. We do it to be competitive.*

As a result of the focus on Six Sigma and other McNerney initiatives, the company has become far more consistent in its ability to execute. But if there is one consistent criticism among McNerney watchers, it is that his intense focus on the bottom line is incompatible with a culture of genuine innovation. At 3M, people were (and are) proud of their tradition of "sideways technology," meaning their ability to leverage and exploit the company's own technology into new products.

So the question that many 3M watchers have asked is this: Can a tightly run McNerney/3M ship, employing the rigorous Six Sigma program as its chief navigational aid, continue the company's tradition of sideways technology?

McNerney claims to understand this danger. He says that the last thing he wants to do is stifle the innovative spirit that brought the world Scotch tape and Post-it notes. He understood from day one, he says, that preserving 3M's unique culture would play a major role in rejuvenating the company.

For example, to emphasize the importance he places on a steady stream of new ideas and innovations, McNerney came up with his "2x/3x challenge." This challenge stated that henceforth, 3M-ers had to double the number of new ideas at the front end of the innovation process and triple the number of "winners" coming out the back end.

To make this challenge a reality, 3M will need to enhance its idea generation process and also find a systematic method for converting ideas into new products that will stand the test of time.

Experts contend that McNerney's 2x/3x plan has the potential to transform the company. By ramping up "knowledge sharing and knowledge management" throughout the company, the plan could help spur productivity in other parts of the business as well, such as in sales and marketing.

In addition to exhorting his idea people, McNerney also puts his money where his mouth is. 3M invests heavily in R&D, spending more than $1.1 billion a year on ensuring the company's future. But he is selective in these investments. One key feature of his productivity plan is to concentrate R&D in those businesses and products that are likely to yield the greatest commercial results. In the past, 3M was not as strategic in its research allocation and expenditures.

Here McNerney evokes the primacy-of-the-customer lesson that became part of the Welch doctrine while adding his own thoughts on innovation:

> *The best and most sustainable innovation occurs where creativity and customer needs intersect. Good ideas don't just leap out of laboratories—they are called out by the clear voice of the customer and need to be reinforced with the right resources.*

An organization's culture is often one of the hardest aspects of corporate life to pin down. (Michael Dell said of culture that he "knows it when he sees it.") Despite its elusive nature, its importance is fully appreciated by the most seasoned of business leaders. They tinker with the "cultural formula" carefully because they can't afford to put the good aspects of the existing culture at risk while they're working on the bad. McNerney understands this: "I think we're world-class at the front end of the innovation process, [so] if I dampen our enthusiasm for that, I've really screwed it up."

Let People Roam Free

It is one thing to pay lip service to "the clear voice of the customer" and quite another to create a culture that helps people to hear that voice through all the noise and clutter inherent in large companies. But McNerney is serious about maintaining an organization that thrives on coming up with the next great new thing—*as defined by the customer*, of course.

One way he helps to foster innovation and keep researchers in touch with their in-house customers is through his "15 percent time" program. This is a forward-looking policy that encourages lab workers to spend up to 15 percent of their time meeting with members of other divisions of the organization and generally canvassing the halls for input from colleagues:

3M values individual ideas, and what I aim to do is preserve that natural tendency for scientists to walk down the hall.

Once again, we see GE's influence on McNerney's 3M. In his final years at GE, Welch became intensely focused on new ideas and on building the "intellect" of the organization. This reflects an interesting evolution in Welch's thinking. Earlier on, he saw "bigness" almost exclusively as a liability. Bigness meant bureaucracy, slow decision making, command and control, and the stifling of innovation.

As noted, however, Welch's thinking on this topic evolved. In his final years at the helm, he began making the point that bigness could be an advantage. Larger companies, he decided, have more people, more brains, and (by extension) more fresh ideas. The challenge is to make sure that there is an operating system in place that is capable of harnessing all that intellect. Of course, "walking the halls" does not an operating system make, but it's certainly true that informal dialogue and discussion, the kind that take place every day in the halls and copy rooms of major companies, are where some of the most meaningful exchanges take place.

HOST INTERDEPARTMENTAL GET-TOGETHERS

In dysfunctional organizations, marketing people rarely talk to manufacturing people, and salespeople hardly ever talk to marketing managers. One way to improve things and encourage innovation is to bring people from different parts of the company together. You might be surprised by the ideas that come out of even the most informal of meetings.

Walking the halls and swapping ideas in copy rooms may sound pedestrian. But it has already led to several significant new products at 3M—some long before McNerney's arrival at the company. McNerney insists that Post-it notes, for example, came about by having 3M scientists do just that. The nanotechnology people got together with the adhesive people, and the rest is history: "The adhesives in Post-its is like the Holy Grail of adhesives," McNerney decreed in early 2004.

How can the rest of us, those who don't manage multibillion-dollar companies, bring the equivalent of "walking the halls" to our own organizations? Consider the following ideas.

The 4E Leader To-Do List

☐ **Combine command and control with a more nurturing style.** McNerney says that the two styles are not incompatible. In fact, he says that you can't have one without the other. When he says "command and control," he doesn't mean that a manager should sit atop a mountain shouting down orders. He means that leaders should not be afraid to make decisions and expect people to carry them out. But he also believes that forceful leaders need to take an interest in their people, and contribute to their professional development.

☐ **Establish a new unit or an ad-hoc task force to tackle new challenges, products, or markets.** Like the kinds of informal get-togethers mentioned earlier, establishing new units or task forces to tackle different challenges or come up with new-product ideas can help ignite innovation. This idea can be particularly useful in large, Old Economy companies that are slumping under the weight of their own bureaucracy.

☐ **Develop a "single language" to boost productivity.** Whether that language be Six Sigma or some other key initiative, it is vital for leaders to make sure that all are operating out of the same playbook. This seems intuitive, perhaps obvious, but many organizations unknowingly add to confusion with the "menu" approach to learning and training. That's what 3M did prior to McNerney by offering multiple quality programs.

☐ **Banish formality so that anyone in the organization feels free to send an e-mail to the CEO.** Most large companies have a strict command structure and insist that everyone stay within the chain of command. But such a rigid hierarchy can stifle innovation and keep the most important information from the people who need it the most. Unless everyone in your firm feels free to send an e-mail to senior management, there is always the chance that the best ideas will never have the chance to bubble up from the bottom.

☐ **Allocate resources where they can do the most good.** This may sound self-evident. But, in fact, many organizations throw good money after bad by trying to "fix" underperforming units or product lines. Meanwhile, as McNerney points out, the best ideas "don't just leap out of laboratories." They require customer input and the right resources. Consider changing the allocation of your R&D resources based on what the marketplace tells you.

CHAPTER 7

EXECUTION IS EVERYTHING

How Larry Bossidy Makes Things Happen

*I get more satisfaction from seeing things get done
than I do about philosophizing or building sand castles.
Many people regard execution as detail work that's
beneath the dignity of a business leader. That's
wrong. It's a leader's most important job.*

—LARRY BOSSIDY, former CEO and
Chairman of the Board, Honeywell

Jack Welch met Larry Bossidy over a Ping-Pong table at a GE management meeting in Hawaii in 1978. In Welch's memoir, he described how the two became engulfed in a no-holds-barred game that helped convince Welch that Bossidy was a glowing exception to the "lackluster" middle managers that filled GE's ranks in the late 1970s.

Welch wrote that he "was excited by this guy who was so full of life and so competitive." Welch would later come to regard Bossidy as "a star" and a "business soul mate." But Welch—and GE—very nearly lost Bossidy even before he really got going.

Right after that "die-to-the-finish" Ping-Pong game, Bossidy shocked Welch with a confession: He said that he was about to leave GE. He simply couldn't *take it* any more, by which he meant all the red tape, procedures, delays, bureaucracies, and other clanking machinery associated with large, lumbering companies. "This place is driving me *nuts*," Bossidy concluded.

Welch fired right back. "Give me a chance," he pleaded. "You're just what we need. This is going to be a different place."

Welch kept his word. GE became a very different place very quickly. Welch promoted Bossidy to chief operating officer of GE Credit before making him vice chairman in 1984—a post that made him the second most influential GE executive. As a result, Bossidy was at Welch's right hand when Welch brought in consultants to help pen the GE values that would form the nucleus of his cultural transformation.

Noel Tichy, the GE consultant who ran Crotonville back then, explained in his book on Welch the goal that confronted him and his team in the mid-1980s: "The challenge of the new Crotonville team was to clear away the last remnants of the old methods while developing programs that exemplified GE's new ideas." "Tearing down the old" is often the first essential step in any change effort, but it is almost always more difficult than most managers believe.

Shortly after the GE values were written, Bossidy found himself eyeball to eyeball with a new managers' class at Crotonville. This came smack in the middle of the most painful part of the Welch era—in the midst of all the divestitures and bloodletting.

Welch claimed, famously, that he didn't fire more than 100,000 employees (the track record that earned him his "Neutron Jack" moniker); he only "fired the positions." But the *effect* was surely the same. The survivors were scared about their futures and angry with their company's leaders—and every other negative emotion in between.

All of those emotions played themselves out at Crotonville that Monday morning in October 1985, as Bossidy stood down in the hot seat (or the "pit," as it is called at Crotonville). One brave new manager had the temerity to ask GE's number-two executive the one question that was on everyone's mind: "What about job security?" Bossidy knew that his answer was critical. In fact, his response most likely would be interpreted as a distillation of both the Welch philosophy and the new GE.

Before facing that class, Tichy had asked Bossidy if he wanted a briefing, knowing that he almost certainly would field some very tough questions. But Crotonville was not open to outsiders, such as journalists or analysts, so it was the one place where Bossidy and Welch felt totally free to speak their minds. So Bossidy told Tichy that no, he didn't need anything; he would simply "go in and interact."

Here's how he handled the job-security question:

> *You're right to raise this. It's an extremely tough issue,*
> *and very relevant. We think the only way to handle this*
> *is to tell people that there is no job security at GE—*
> *other than what the customer can provide. . . . That's*
> *the reality of the marketplace.*

In delivering those words, Bossidy proved that he was a leader with edge and (as it turned out) the ability to energize others. This was a new brand of candor. Before Welch and Bossidy, this was not the kind of exchange that would have been heard in any GE hall or training center. But this was exactly the kind of honesty that was needed within the century-old company. Like so many other sprawling bureaucracies, it had grown content, and contentment is the enemy of continuous improvement.

Bossidy concluded that meeting with a heartfelt plea. He explained that he "passionately believed" in the GE values but that at the same time, he knew that some of the managers in the room didn't share his passion. He challenged his new managers to decide where they stood. If, in their hearts, they did not subscribe to the GE values, they should "make the decision to get out." In other words, Bossidy's own convictions on

HELP YOUR PEOPLE TO SEE THINGS FOR WHAT THEY ARE

When Bossidy told those managers that there was "no job security other than what the customer can provide," he was forcing them to look squarely at the truth. Welch called this "facing reality," and it was his first rule of business. Too many managers have their heads in the sand. They don't confront reality. They let underperformers stay on the payroll because they are comfortable with the status quo and hate confrontation. By telling that class the truth, Bossidy was instilling trust while simultaneously challenging those managers to upgrade their performance. A note of caution: Don't expect candor unless you are prepared to consistently dole it out. And if you dole it out, be prepared to get it back.

this score overlapped almost entirely with Welch's: You are either on the bus or off the bus. If you're off the bus, get out. It was a risky kind of candor but again (as it turned out) an engaging one. Tichy, Bossidy, and the management class came away from that encounter feeling truly energized.

Create Change Agents

As Jack Welch's vice chairman, Bossidy played a major role during Welch's tenure as head of GE. He was a strong number two and a very effective counterpoint to Welch. It was Welch who declared Crotonville to be the headquarters for GE's transformation, for example, but it was Bossidy who spoke up for the thousands of GE middle managers who were not invited to the prestigious campus on the Hudson.

Former Crotonville head Noel Tichy called Bossidy "an instinctive populist." The GE vice chairman was an *inclusive* manager who sought to involve as many managers as possible in the change effort. As a result, GE started to host management workshops in distant destinations—such as Gotemba, Japan— that brought together executives from many of GE's far-flung businesses.

In most change efforts, it is middle management that winds up doing most of the heavy lifting. Middle managers are closer to the front lines and to the people who do all the work. Unless they are equipped to deliver the company goal, mission, values, and so on to their employees effectively, a change effort is very likely to fail.

Transformation efforts also will fail if the message of top management is not in alignment with the message all the way down the line. That is why it is critical to make middle managers partners in any large-scale transformation.

Bossidy understood both these principles. He therefore sought to include middle managers more actively and to educate them and secure their buy-in. As a result, according to Noel Tichy, approximately half of the training that took place at GE in the 1980s was done *outside* of Crotonville. Reaching out to a broader base of managers helped to drive the GE executioncentric culture deeper into the fabric of the organization. It also made GE more agile and better able to deal with the seismic shifts that were occurring in the marketplace.

These workshops had a very specific purpose: to help transform managers into change agents while working on concrete and specific strategies and solutions to help the company. For example, in that Gotemba course, one of the challenges was to come up with new ways for the Power Systems business (which had been selling fewer turbines in the United States) to attract new customers in Asia.

In order to make these sessions as meaningful as possible, the number of participants was limited to a relatively small number; at Gotemba, for instance, there were 30 attendees, divided up into six 5-person teams. The sessions were very carefully thought out.

For example, prominent professors from universities like Harvard (as well as top Japanese universities) were invited to discuss strategy and global marketing. Managers engaged in "visioning" exercises in order to understand how a specific vision can influence future events (Martin Luther King's "I Have a Dream" speech was one prominent example used).

TURN MANAGERS INTO CHANGE AGENTS

To transform an organization's culture from passive to more executioncentric, you will need to energize as many people as possible. The most lasting and meaningful change occurs when change is driven from the bottom up, as well as from the top down. But that can happen only when employees and managers understand the vision and the goals and are rewarded for hitting key targets. Too many organizations tolerate "wanderers" and "dabblers"—employees who do not understand how their contributions fit into the rest of the company and therefore are relatively ineffectual contributors.

In order to give middle managers an understanding of how they, and their units, fit into the overall scheme of things, a senior GE organizational planning manager was invited to give participants the wider view. Such sessions helped to put the company's entire change effort into perspective while showing managers how their small piece of the company contributed to the performance of the whole.

Hold Managers Accountable

Of course, to really change the business, Bossidy and Welch had to do more than school managers at workshops and at Crotonville. Deep structural changes were required. (This was the period when *delayering* and *downsizing* became watchwords at GE.) In an effort to simplify the organization and instill greater ownership, the company had gotten rid of its strategic planning staff within two years of Welch's appointment as CEO. Both Welch and Bossidy felt strongly that strategy was integral to the manager's job:

> *A separate planning function can undermine the objective because it permits the manager to sidestep the issue, and it promotes isolation. Don't give the manager a planner. Rather, demand a comprehensive strategy review within six months of the manager's assignment.*

By taking away the planners, the company was taking away the "crutch" that had stood between the leaders and their businesses. It was, in effect, forcing managers to face reality and to devise strategies based on that reality. By holding managers more accountable, GE was instilling more ownership into all of the management ranks.

These sorts of structural changes—in conjunction with the shared values, the workshops, and the Crotonville courses—had the effect of making the company better conditioned, better prepared, and most of all, better at delivering results. They helped build a company that had execution "in its blood."

There are many ways to build more accountability into the organization. Consider implementing one or more of the following:

■ *Ask direct reports to come up with their own annual stretch targets.* Employees who participate in their own personal development plans will feel more like partners than like employees. This will also help you to secure buy-in and add incentives for employees to go the extra mile in achieving those goals.

■ *Reward the results that matter most.* Many companies have archaic incentive plans that do not directly link rewards with the contributions that matter most. Review your company's incentive plans to ensure that payouts are directly linked to the precise results that will make the most difference.

■ *Reinforce accountability in company values, communications, training, and so on.* Accountability needs to be consistently reinforced by senior management. Incorporate it into the key activities and operating system. Do not be afraid to tell managers and employees alike that ownership and accountability will be the new order of things, and make sure that that message makes its way to every corner of the company.

Writing the Book on Execution

Bossidy remained a staunch friend of Welch even after he left GE to run AlliedSignal and, later, Honeywell (the company that Welch tried in vain to acquire in 2000). At AlliedSignal, Bossidy learned of the quality program Six Sigma and told Welch that if Welch implemented it at GE, he would "write the book on quality." Welch took his friend at his word, implemented the program with a vengeance, and made Six Sigma the hottest management initiative since reengineering.

With a push from Bossidy, therefore, Welch got to "write the book on quality." But it was Bossidy himself who got to write the book on execution. *Execution: The Discipline of Getting Things Done* was coauthored with author and consultant Ram Charan, and it went on to become number one on the *New York Times* best-seller list in 2002. Bossidy, the protégé, had emerged as a leading management voice and best-selling author:

> *Leaders who can't execute don't get free runs anymore.*
> *Execution is the great unaddressed business issue in*
> *the business world today.*

Bossidy and Charan explained that execution was the new currency that would separate authentic leaders from the also-rans. Only through forging a genuine, execution-oriented culture, they argued, could leaders build real credibility. Bossidy and Charan also described the following three vital points on execution, and its importance to any organization's success:

> *Execution is a discipline, and integral to strategy.*
>
> *Execution is the major job of the business leader.*
>
> *Execution must be a core element of an organization's culture.*

If you look more closely at these three statements, something interesting emerges: They're all about *consistency*. Execution can't be something that happens once in a while. It is a discipline, a core element, the major job of the leader—and, as it turns out, of *everybody*.

Bossidy also pointed out that execution, like other company-wide initiatives such as Six Sigma, will only bear fruit if the

DEVELOP AN "ARCHITECTURE FOR EXECUTION"

Execution must be integral to everything a company does, an overriding theme that permeates the organization's culture. Execution needs to be a reflex, something that becomes second nature. Make execution a prominent part of the incentive system, as well as a primary criterion for promotions. That will happen only if you incorporate it into goals, assignments, training, annual reviews, and everything else.

company trains for execution and allows its people to "practice it constantly." He also notes that it will not take root unless a company trains the majority of its people in it.

To make sure that execution is ingrained in every corner of an organization, the leaders of the organization must keep it front and center at all times. Stated slightly differently, the responsibility for ensuring that execution remains a key company priority lies with senior management. It cannot be delegated, and it must be addressed on many different levels simultaneously:

Having an execution discipline is about getting the job done . . . but with a broad systematic view—one that integrates the mission objective with the tools, the metrics, the people, and the processes that will get you there. Quite simply, organizations that can't execute fall by the wayside.

169

Use Metrics and Measurements

During the marketing campaign for his book, Bossidy explained in an interview that accountability is one of the real keys to effective cultural transformation. He also espoused his deep-seated belief in measurement, which played a decisive role in his success throughout his 34-year career:

> *Change can't occur without laser-like accountability and metrics to measure how you are doing. I encourage organizations to measure their financial performance against two-year plans.*

As mentioned in Part 1, it was Bossidy who convinced Welch that Six Sigma—which is all about metrics and measurements— was the real thing ("no b.s." was the way he described it to his former boss). Bossidy learned about the statistically based quality program when he defected to AlliedSignal in 1991.

However, implementing Six Sigma was the last thing Welch wanted to do. He had seen his share of management whims and fads—from quality circles to reengineering—and he was not keen to launch headlong into an initiative that might crash and burn. But Bossidy's persuasiveness, and his long-standing credibility with Welch, won the day.

After being convinced by Bossidy that Six Sigma would be a powerful tool for GE, Welch invited Bossidy back to GE to make a presentation to his management team, which included many of Bossidy's former colleagues. (Before Welch, it should be noted, it was not a common practice for one CEO to invite a potential competitor to address the senior-level troops.) Again, in that context, Bossidy hammered away at his central conviction:

If you don't measure it, it doesn't get done.

Six Sigma, Bossidy told the assembled GE brass, measures things in a way that *ensures* that things get done. By all accounts, he was persuasive, but it can be inferred that his audience was predisposed to believe in the power of measurement. After all, Bossidy had learned about the power of metrics during his *own* years at GE, when Welch set specific targets for improving productivity, inventory returns, net income, and of course, the company's stock price and capitalization. Bossidy was not just "coming home"; he was preaching to the choir.

When Bossidy took over AlliedSignal, he faced many of his own problems, and there were no overnight quick fixes. Change efforts would require years of hard work before they yielded substantial dividends. He also had to change the mind-set of the organization, getting people to "question everything."

Years later, after it was announced that AlliedSignal was to merge with Honeywell, Bossidy wanted to be sure that the combined company didn't lose the momentum that he had built at AlliedSignal. To ensure that this did not happen, he assigned AlliedSignal's vice president of Six Sigma and productivity as one of two executives in charge of the integration team:

> *Six Sigma has been successful at Honeywell because we are committed to ensuring it permeates every nook and cranny of the organization. We make Six Sigma metrics and evaluations part of every leader's semiannual management talent reviews.*

Bossidy also insisted that Six Sigma be integrated into each unit's operating plans, and he made sure that each unit supplied him with progress reports. He was as passionate as Welch about driving

Six Sigma down into the organization to create better leaders in every unit. Bossidy never took his eye off the ball. He told all constituencies (shareholders, employees, and managers) that Six Sigma would be the primary engine fueling "six percent productivity improvement forever."

Confirming and institutionalizing or sustaining process improvements is critical to the success of our Six Sigma efforts.

In the end, all the hard work, all the measurements, and all the investments in Six Sigma helped Bossidy turn the company around. At AlliedSignal, earnings per share grew at a healthy double-digit rate (13 percent plus) for 31 quarters in a row. One of the driving forces behind's Bossidy's success was his ability to rally the company around the needs of the customer. Those results were impressive enough to attract suitor Honeywell, which acquired the company in 1999—and named Bossidy as its chairman.

The 4E Leader To-Do List

☐ **Drive training down into the depths of the organization.** In launching any change initiative, you will need as much help as possible to make sure that the message reaches the far corners of the organization. The more managers you can enlist in the effort, the better. This means inculcating both the values and the competencies throughout the management ranks.

☐ **Ask all your business leaders to come up with a six-month plan.** There must be accountability in the organization in order for senior managers to remain credible and maintain the confidence of the organization. By getting six-month plans from your leaders, you will have a much better idea of what is working, who is working, and what adjustments need to be made.

☐ **Take a "broad systematic view" of the organization.** To get an organization to execute consistently, many things must be in alignment simultaneously. Bossidy explains that all the following variables must be in synch: mission, metrics, tools, people, and processes. A weak link in any of these important execution components means that the company's ability to execute may be hampered.

CHAPTER 8

ENHANCE, EXTEND, EXPAND

How Robert Nardelli Gave Home Depot a Makeover

*Our core purpose is to improve everything we touch.
Underneath that core purpose is a strategy that talks
about enhancing the core, extending the business, and
expanding our markets. . . . Those three are kind
of chiseled in granite and are timeless."*

—ROBERT NARDELLI, CEO, Home Depot

It was one of the last places you might expect to find the leader of the Free World.

In late 2003, George W. Bush popped up in (of all places) a Home Depot in suburban Halethorp, Maryland. Standing beside the forty-third president of the United States was Robert Nardelli, CEO of Home Depot, the thirteenth-largest company in the United States.

Nardelli is no stranger to chief executives—whether of companies, states, or nations. A diehard Republican and an unabashed Bush supporter, Nardelli has made at least three treks to the

White House. During one of those visits, President Bush paid tribute to the Home Depot CEO for supporting his employees who had been sent to Iraq.

Rubbing elbows with presidents—not a bad outcome for the other guy (along with James McNerney) who didn't get Jack Welch's job. In late 2000, after Welch picked Jeff Immelt, Home Depot snapped up Nardelli almost overnight (Nardelli says, "It took a week"), making him the first outsider to run the company in its 20-plus-year history. It didn't seem to matter that Nardelli had no retail or direct consumer experience. Like so many companies that are founded by visionaries, Home Depot had outgrown its infrastructure and was in desperate need of a strong, capable admiral to right the ship.

Nardelli enjoyed a sterling reputation, having grown GE Power Systems from a $6 billion business into a $15 billion business within five years. Welch contended that in his 40 years with GE, no other executive had ever delivered better numbers. He went so far as to declare that Nardelli's financial performance was the best of any manager in GE's history—including his own!

Nardelli spent nearly three decades at GE, holding more than a dozen different leadership positions, before making the move to Home Depot.

As Power Systems CEO, Nardelli's final GE post, he acquired 50 companies and multiplied profits by a staggering 700 percent. Remarks GE's top HR executive, Bill Conaty, "Jack and I used to marvel at his ability to execute."

The Fifth E?

To marvel "at his ability to execute." That is an apt way to describe the reaction to Nardelli and his accomplishments. In his almost three decades at GE, he held numerous leadership positions, and each time he answered the call by blowing away his numbers and, along with them, all expectations. When in 2005 he was asked how he specifically he used the 4E's—both at GE and at Home Depot—he cautioned that they should not be the be-all-and-end-all of leadership. But he also revealed a very intriguing fact regarding the 4E's:

> *I added a couple of E's. . . . I have added an E called execution, and since I have been at Home Depot I have added another E called endurance. . . . I remember we only close two days a year . . . that's on Thanksgiving Day and Christmas Day, so endurance becomes another very important E in retailing.*

Remember that Welch wrote there were *only three* E's at first and that a fourth E was added later. Could it be that it was Robert Nardelli, and not Jack Welch, who added the fourth E? That would be more than a little ironic, since it is Welch who is credited with all four of the E's, and it was Larry Bossidy who cowrote the best-selling book entitled *Execution*.

In any event, no one argues that Nardelli was a business leader with the kind of proven track record that would impress anyone. And he certainly typified all five E's, including his own addition—endurance (he was at GE almost 30 years, joining the company during the Nixon administration). Home Depot is open 363 days a year, meaning that it is open whenever someone wants to shop there. That same "our doors are always open" attitude is also one of the success factors behind the world's largest retailer, Wal-Mart. (In an interview with this author in 2003, former Wal-Mart CEO David Glass said that that was one of the reasons his company has been so successful, particularly when compared with smaller stores that close their doors on weekends.)

What was the secret to Nardelli's unmitigated success? In an interview with the author's representative in the winter of 2005, Nardelli described his GE training in glowing terms: "I was afforded a tremendous amount of opportunities at GE to learn a variety of businesses and a variety of markets." Nardelli added that he was the recipient of "the best professional and educational environment that one could have." What did all that training accomplish?

> *What I learned was the ability to assess a business, a market an industry and put together a very cohesive and actionable strategy that created an inspirational vision for the men and women in the organization.*

Remarkably, Nardelli led 13 different businesses at GE. As the GE succession race unfolded, it became increasingly clear that the two candidates who did *not* get the top job at GE would more or less have their pick of any CEO opening in corporate America—and might even be offered some jobs that were not so open. Once Welch realized this, he did something unprecedented: He told each of the three that if he did not get the job, he would be *forced* to leave GE.

Then he told them that in order to make the coming transitions as seamless as possible, each needed to train his successor CEOs for six months. (At GE, the head of each major business segment holds the title of CEO.) And then Welch announced publicly who those three "junior CEOs" would be.

What was Welch thinking? First, he understood that there was a 99 percent chance that the two who didn't get the nod would leave, no matter what. (No capable and competitive executive on that level wants to hang around after having been passed over—and these individuals wouldn't need to.)

But Welch was also thinking of GE's best interests, as he saw them. The high-profile succession race for the top job was unsettling the company. Welch was determined to counter all the buzzing and speculation by at least settling the three "smaller" succession races that his own departure might ignite. To succeed Immelt, McNerney, and Nardelli, he settled on three A executives who were, coincidentally, all 43 years old at the time:

> *Putting these three stars into these new jobs was a game-changing event. While 300,000 employees, including me, still didn't know who their chairman was going to be, the people in three of our biggest businesses knew exactly who their new CEOs would be.*

Nardelli, like McNerney, found out he hadn't gotten Welch's job from Welch himself. The GE chief, who eschewed the GE jet in favor of a chartered plane, flew secretly to each of the three's hometowns to deliver the news in person. Nardelli could not believe that Welch hadn't picked him. "I want an autopsy," he snapped at Welch.

Moments after GE announced that it was Immelt who would succeed Welch, Nardelli got a call from GE board member and Home Depot insider Ken Langone. "You probably could not feel worse right now, but you've just been hit in the ass with a golden horseshoe. And I've got the horseshoe." But it quickly became clear that Home Depot wasn't the only company in the hunt for Nardelli. Kodak, Ford, and Lucent emerged as suitors as well.

In *less* than seven days, Home Depot made room for Nardelli by pushing its CEO and cofounder Arthur Blank out of his CEO post. Like the ambitious son who has been told by his father that he is good, but not quite *good enough*, Nardelli has been engaged in a furious exercise of demonstrating that *he* was, and is, the pick of the Welch litter. (For the record, Nardelli denies that this motivates him.)

THE 4E LEADER DEVELOPS SUCCESSION PLANS FOR KEY TOP MANAGEMENT POSTS

By telling the three candidates that they would have to train their successors, Welch was getting each of them to face reality while safeguarding the future of GE. Don't delegate succession or leave it to chance or to the last minute. The best managers start thinking, and actively planning, for their own successors—and the successors of their key managers—years in advance.

However, there is no doubt that he has the work ethic. In his new job, Nardelli makes it a practice to arrive at his office at the crack of dawn (6:15 a.m.)—and often stays until 9:00 p.m. Even Nardelli's predecessor, Arthur Blank, cannot believe how hard Nardelli works. Says Blank of Nardelli's hard-charging ways: "It's not a job. It's a life."

Connect the Dots

In late 2004, *BusinessWeek* pointed out what most experts already knew: "Under Jack Welch, GE developed the deepest bench of executive talent in U.S. business." Nardelli was a key piece of that calculation. He started at GE in 1971, and later—as CEO of Power Systems—built that unit into a thriving, global leader in the energy industry.

He did it by expanding the business into services—by providing product and service *solutions*—while also creating a host of new products. (Under his leadership, the unit introduced 50 percent more new products and services.) His GE background served him exceedingly well in his new CEO position. By leaving GE, however, he brought something to Home Depot that that he could not have brought to the GE boardroom: an outsider's perspective. It was that perspective that helped him to create new businesses and business models at the home retailing giant.

For example, as Nardelli explained in early 2005: "We weren't in the Home Depot supply business four years ago. Now its growing about 30, 35 percent a year. . . . through organic and inorganic initiatives we have broadened our portfolio of merchandise, and we are now serving customers we otherwise would not have served, so that the breadth of our offering now more mirror images a broader market opportunity not only from a product standpoint but more mirror imaging our customer base."

Nardelli did things the GE way by placing a high premium on leadership development and succession planning, spending more than $600 million on training and clocking 23 million hours of learning in 2004 alone. Nardelli also established three distinct leadership programs: an executive leadership program, an advanced leadership program, and a store leadership program. But the real story of Nardelli's reinvention of the company is about firing on all cylinders simultaneously. In early 2005, Nardelli spoke of just what it took to lead a business successfully in today's increasingly complex, global marketplace:

> *...the ability to connect the dots...look at a market and assess megatrends, the ability to see the future or the economy the way it is, and therefore, put in place initiatives or actionable items that allowed us to persevere through economic cycles, global unrest, currency fluctuations and so forth.*

Overhaul the "Cowboy Culture"

Like many great companies, Home Depot was founded by a visionary CEO with plenty of charisma (Bernie Marcus); he also had a strong numbers man to back him up (Arthur Blank).

The two men founded Home Depot in 1978 as a "builder's supply store for the rest of us." The company caught fire from the start.

Within three years, Home Depot went public, and by 1984, the company had just over 30 stores delivering well over $400 million in sales. By 1996, the company had achieved a remarkable feat: 40 quarters in a row of record growth and profits. During the 1990s, Home Depot's stock market value increased an eye-popping 3,700 percent.

By 2000, however, the company had been pummeled by eight straight quarters of dwindling growth. Customer service was lagging, and the huge orange "big box" stores that were the company's trademark were beginning to resemble cluttered warehouses. This and other operational lapses were helping rivals to make inroads on the retailing giant's home turf.

Wal-Mart, for example, was sneaking up on Home Depot with rock-bottom prices, and Lowe's, the number-two player in the market, was successfully attacking Home Depot at the high end and whittling away Home Depot's market share. Lowe's was doing a better job of appealing to women and families. And there were more fundamental problems at Home Depot as well. Each orange-box store was an island unto itself. Store managers didn't communicate with one another, and they were not even connected by e-mail! This meant that there were separate buying functions, different pricing strategies, and so on.

In other words, decentralization was killing the company. The "Generals"—General Motors and General Electric—were among the first to use decentralization as an organizing principle after World War II. But the model, which had its virtues in that postwar era, also spawned layers of bureaucracy to help the company "manage" the far-flung units and divisions.

By the 1980s, in the eyes of most observers, the decentralization experiment had run its course, and the model had outlived its usefulness. In the early 2000s, Home Depot was desperate to find a way to "pull itself together"—literally.

For instance, Home Depot had nine different regional offices and a decentralized buying policy to go with them, which meant that the company was not taking advantage of its size and its tremendous buying power. "It was like having nine different wives," remarked one midwestern toolmaker.

This "cowboy culture" (so dubbed by Patricia Sellers at *Fortune*) had many other manifestations. Inventories were piling up, especially in the face of the mounting recession. The company was drowning in paper. One former Home Depot manager said that he would receive a call, an e-mail, a memo, and a fax—all regarding the same subject. Another manager literally wallpapered his office—ceiling, floors, walls, and windows—with about 21 days' worth of the blizzard of missives he received from various directions.

When Nardelli was told about the paperwork run amok in the spring of 2003, he took decisive action. He eliminated unnecessary redundancies, and he purchased $2 million of workload-management software. He had helped Jack Welch rid GE of red tape, and he was determined to inject the same sort of take-no-prisoners, can-do attitude at Home Depot. Nardelli's rhetoric—and play book—built on what he had learned at GE. For example:

...we have tried to create here an environment that encourages and continues to foster an entrepreneurial spirit but at the same time is bringing a process and metric accountability to our programs and our initiatives.

He was also hell-bent on reducing redundancies, overlaps, and overkills. For example, Nardelli learned that his new company had no fewer than 157 different performance appraisal forms. By mid-2002, the company had only two, which together covered all 300,000 Home Depot managers and employees. But Nardelli was also learning the hard way that many of the things that had made the company so effective in its early years were now working against it:

It is a company that has grown up with its cofounders. But my assessment was that it wouldn't get us where we wanted to go in the future. We had a very decentralized business. What I found was that the fundamental infrastructure needed for sustainability in a variety of economic cycles was missing.

A big challenge facing anyone who tried to transform Home Depot, or any other large organization, was to change the culture. To achieve meaningful change, Nardelli would have to reach beyond the senior ranks and influence the many thousands of managers and employees who made up the heart of the company: "We now communicate regularly all the way down to the stores. And there's an ever-increasing understanding and embracing of the that strategy and core purpose."

Nardelli understood that to realize meaningful cultural change and instill a productivity-driven mind-set throughout the company, he would have to give managers and employees alike the tools and training they needed to pull it off. Like any effective leader, he understood that the best strategy in the world is useless without the right kind of people to implement it. He made a habit of spending increasing amounts of time in the field with his business leaders, digging down deep into the organization in an effort to strengthen the company, its competencies, and spread Best Practices:

> *We'll talk about succession planning. We have put in place since I have been here a store manager forum where we get every store manager in the company together. We have put it in for the assistant store managers, for the district managers, for the regional vice-presidents. So we've really tried to create a very transparent organization focusing heavily on alignment, focusing heavy on a culture that allows people to listen, and then learn to launch.*

Although Nardelli and Home Depot hit a few bumps in the early days, Nardelli's leadership has helped to turn the ship around. In part because he was not wedded to the past, he was able to make the tough decisions that were needed to put Home Depot on the right track.

Simple Strategies Work Best

Nardelli reinvented the company the GE way. He recognized immediately that the company was behaving like a loosely knit confederation rather than like a Fortune 50 company. It had enormous clout on both the purchasing and the marketing ends that it was simply leaving on the table.

Nardelli wasted little time in implementing his makeover. He put in centralized vendor agreements. He transformed operations. He replaced most of the senior management team, and he flattened the organizational structure. (Welch had done the same thing at GE.) Nardelli's strategy was anything but complex, and could be articulated in nine words:

Our strategy was very simple. Enhance the core. Extend the business. Expand the market. . . . You have to look at who is first in each category and then figure out how to beat them.

Nardelli had some very specific ideas and initiatives associated with each component of his strategy:

Enhance the core. Nardelli spent more than $10 billion on technology to spark productivity and bring the company's antiquated information systems into the new century. Some of that was used for inventory management systems and in-store Internet-based kiosks that offered customers thousands of special-order products. To better compete with Lowe's, he offered higher-margin products, thus increasing the average dollars per purchase.

Extend the business. New stores, new formats, and new businesses would help fuel growth, argued Nardelli. In 2003, Home Depot added 175 new stores and added more net new jobs than any other established U.S. corporation. Training was also a top priority, and company associates received more than 21 million hours of training.

Expand the market. Nardelli also reached beyond U.S. borders. By the end of 2003, the company had more than one hundred stores in Canada (with plans for more), stores in Mexico, and plans to expand in China and other high-growth markets. The company is also aggressively pursuing homebuilders and other professionals, including maintenance and repair professionals, as distinct growth markets.

> ## THE 4E LEADER DEVELOPS A SOUND, CUSTOMER-BASED STRATEGY AND STICKS TO IT
>
> Nardelli is a leader who sticks to his guns. He spoke with pride of his tri-tiered plan in 2005: "Under each of those three of enhance, extend and expand, the dynamics of the market and the customer will shape the initiatives of distinction and innovative merchandising, for example, store readiness digitization . . . all of those under the core which will result in same store sales improvement, sales per square foot productivity."

It's People Who Do the Executing

One of the key initiatives was Nardelli's human resource initiative, called SOAR, "Strategic Operating and Resource Planning." Nardelli learned long ago that the key to "operationalizing" any strategy is "through human resource." Home Depot then "put in place a series of initiatives starting with a performance matrix that really brought to light both qualitative and quantitative expectations of our leadership team and our associates throughout the organization." Nardelli then installed a number of "learning experiences" and launched a series of leadership programs for executives, managers, store managers, and so on.

By the fall of 2004, more than 800 stores had self-service checkout counters, and every store had been involved in some aspect of the company's modernization effort. Nardelli understands the Drucker dictum of "*structure follows strategy*." He reorganized to better serve the needs of the professional contracting market:

I think you have to identify your strategy and then organize to support it. The real differentiator is resource allocation, both human capital and physical capital. At the leadership level we are going through a major transformation.

The Nardelli strategy ultimately paid strong dividends and helped the company to increase its sales and operating margins. But those successes came later—*much* later, or so it must have seemed to the former GE executive. In fact, Nardelli's first years at his new employer were rocky ones indeed.

The initial glee over his arrival—a Welch protégé!—dissipated all too quickly. The honeymoon was over. Investors lost confidence and began dumping Home Depot shares. Suddenly, the man who was supposed to be the next Jack Welch looked like tainted goods.

That, at least, was the way the press began to talk about Nardelli and Home Depot. But Nardelli was in for the long haul:

I learned from experience. Sometimes you have to fail to win.

Many argued that Nardelli had implemented his changes too quickly. Critics pointed out that Home Depot was not particularly analogous to GE. It was not a "company of companies," nor was consumer retailing anything like the aircraft engine, turbine, or energy businesses. They pointed out that the cultures of GE and Home Depot could hardly be more different. GE had a performance-based culture linked by common values. Home Depot's culture was more freewheeling and independent.

Nardelli was and is convinced that his critics are wrong. When asked by *Fortune* what he would have done differently, he replied:

I wished I had moved faster . . . finding the strategy and being able to bring it to life—I wish I could have done it faster. We were not as quick or as agile as a retailer must be. The modernized stores are performing better than the nonmodernized stores in a market area, so obviously if we could have moved faster, we could have seen results sooner.

Perhaps not coincidentally, *"I wish I had moved faster"* are the exact words Welch used after 17 years at the helm of GE. Welch wished that he had moved faster—faster in making the changes in culture, launching his services initiative, implementing Six Sigma, and so on. Clearly, Nardelli shares Welch's instinct for both speed and change.

Welch and Nardelli have other things in common as well. Most people forget that the press hated Welch in his first years. He was labeled as "un-American" by the *Los Angeles Times* and called "Neutron Jack" by just about everyone else. When he divested the company's Housewares Division in 1984, the *New York Times* commented bitterly that it was "as if General Motors suddenly abandoned car-making." His every move, it seemed, was condemned in the media.

The difficult reality is that it takes years for change efforts to bear fruit in a multibillion-dollar company. And yet, under the harsh glare of the media spotlight, there is increasing pressure on today's CEOs to produce results right out of the gate. Miss an earnings estimate—even by a penny—and Wall Street will punish you for that failure.

For instance, months before Nardelli took over, when then-CEO Arthur Blank warned that Home Depot's earnings would fall short for the year, investors dumped shares so quickly that the stock plummeted 28 percent in a single day—the worst day in Home Depot's history. Although Nardelli has never had *that* bad a day, he's had his share of disappointments. Wall Street has been hard on him and the company's stock price. At one time, Home Depot's stock was down by half under Nardelli.

Once his transformation efforts started to bear fruit, however, the stock rebounded. At one point it more than doubled in less than 18 months.

Being a leader often means making decisions that others call foolish or wrong. It takes edge to stick to your plan when critics hammer you every day. Nardelli has been characterized as being thin-skinned by the media. The quick trigger of Wall Street and the "gotcha" attitude on the part of the press corps rankle him. "The stock price will catch up to the strategy," he contends, and once again he is sticking to his guns. His goal is to make Home Depot a $100 billion company. He understands that the world's largest home-improvement supplies retailer must be reinvented or risk being made irrelevant:

> *The rate of internal change must be greater than the rate of external change, or [we] will fall behind. We have to change the business model. What got us here may not get us there.*

Structure Follows Strategy

One Nardelli strategy was to *extend* the business while simultaneously *expanding* the market. By diving into services and thereby offering Home Depot's customers more than supplies and lumber, the company was tapping into a multi-hundred-billion-dollar business. Nardelli correctly predicted that the millions of customers who shopped in his stores would want installations

THE 4E LEADER REINVENTS
THE ORGANIZATION

Home Depot was in desperate need of an overhaul, but most of the management team did not face up to this fact. Organizations need to be flexible enough to make the necessary changes and adjustments as competitive pressures and the environment dictate. Take a good, long look at your business and its segments every couple of years. Figure out what needs to be changed, and be bold in moving ahead with the changes.

and other services performed for them. He calculated that the "do-it-yourselfers" were turning into the "do-it-for-me's."

Nardelli calculates that the entire home improvement market is about a $900 billion market.

Of that sum, he figures that the installation market exceeds $100 billion and that it tops $300 billion when you add in raw goods and materials. Home Depot now installs everything from roofing to bathrooms to home security systems. It builds decks and sheds; it replaces windows. It will fix your broken appliances and rid your home of pests:

> *Through our service business, we are positioned to capitalize on demographic shifts that are creating customers who want home improvements "done for them." . . . We currently handle more than 10,000 projects each business day and expect this business to continue its double digit growth rate.*

In pursuing services, Nardelli was taking yet another page from the Welch playbook. In the mid-1990s, Welch realized that there was an entirely new business that the company was not exploiting. He called it "Product Services," and that became the second Welch growth initiative (Globalization having been the first).

Other prominent business leaders followed suit in the mid-1990s: for example, former IBM CEO Lou Gerstner made services—and solutions—a prominent part of "Big Blue's" turnaround strategy. Welch credited the service initiative with "broadening our definition of services . . . to a larger and bolder vision." Within five years, Welch had turned his vision into a $17 billion business reality.

When Nardelli got to Home Depot in late 2000, he faced some of the same obstacles that Welch had faced while trying to grow GE in the early 1980s. For one hundred years, GE had been one of the world's great manufacturing companies. The entire company was focused on making things like light bulbs and refrigerators and turbines. As a result, GE had a huge base of customers, but growth in many of its markets was slowing because its customers did not need a new turbine or a new aircraft engine every day (or every year, for that matter).

Part of the answer was to charge GE's customers for some of the things that they had been getting for free. At Home Depot, Nardelli figured that many of the same people who sought home improvements did not know how to put in a sink, paint a house, or install new gutters. Perhaps that was why he called home improvement "the sweet spot of retailing," since few other types of retailers have this sort of opportunity to "upsell" their customers.

It Always Comes Back to the E's

Many continue to criticize Nardelli for attacking cultural transformation with all the finesse of a bull in a china shop. Some managers resent the 8 p.m. weeknight meetings that he occasionally calls—not to mention the 7:30 meetings on Saturday morning. It may or may not be fair to fault a CEO for pushing this hard. You *can* fault him, however, for losing key personnel, as Nardelli did during the first year of his tenure.

Again, Nardelli feels that he made the right decisions, tough as some of them turned out to be. He called the company's merit raises "out of control," and he sought to rein in a company that even its co-founder called "loosey-goosey."

> *I love the entrepreneurial spirit. I just want to have some compliant entrepreneurship spirit at a certain time.*

In almost all cases in which a company is struggling, a CEO has to walk a fine line between pushing too hard and not getting control of the organization. If Nardelli was heavy-handed, especially in the beginning, perhaps he can be forgiven for his zeal. First, that's what he was *hired* to do and be. Even his critics would agree that Home Depot was in dire need of financial and managerial discipline. It needed a leader who was not afraid to tell it like it was and who was able to use hard-nosed metrics to gauge productivity and performance. When he was disparaged for overburdening Home Depot with *too many* metrics, a somewhat irritated Nardelli likened his company to an automobile: "Well, take all the gauges off the car. Why do you need a speedometer?"

And second, Nardelli led by example. He never asked any of his direct reports to work harder than he himself did. Saturday morning meetings were a burden on him as much as on anyone else. But he was convinced that this level of commitment was the only thing that would turn Home Depot around.

Nardelli, like the other exceptional leaders described in this book, understands that winning, ultimately, comes down to people, resource allocation, and the quality of leadership. And despite the tough talk, Nardelli understands that he needs the same type of people who made GE the world's most valuable company:

> *What we're looking for is someone that has demonstrated*
> *a tremendous amount of energy, who has an ability to*
> *energize. . . . In this business, you've got to love people.*
> *We're looking for people who want to continue to learn, who*
> *understand the importance of individual accountability,*
> *but with the ability to think laterally.*

To retain his best people, Nardelli pays his associates an average of 15 percent more than the average community wage. He also has put in an incentive plan that he calls "success sharing." The plan pays associates a bonus when managers hit store sales goals and other key metrics. He takes pride in the fact that in a recent year Home Depot paid associates $16 million through that program.

> *We have a real passion, a real commitment about attracting,*
> *motivating and retaining a high performance workforce.*

The 4E Leader To-Do List

☐ **Enhance the core, extend the business, expand the market.** Nardelli enhanced the core by upgrading the stores; he extended the business by offering installation and other service programs; and he expanded the market by opening new stores in high-growth markets like China. Find ways to enhance your core business while also extending and expanding.

☐ **Move faster.** Jack Welch and Bob Nardelli both wished that they had moved faster to reinvent their companies. Nardelli says that the one thing that keeps him up at night is the speed at which things happen. Consider taking bolder action; don't let fear of the new or unexpected keep you from trying new things or entering new markets.

☐ **Plunge into services and solutions.** When the growth of your manufacturing and other core businesses starts to slow, look to services as a new growth strategy. While not all businesses lend themselves to this strategy, there are many different industries in which services and solutions can help spark double-digit growth.

☐ **Create targeted incentive plans that reward managers for hitting key metrics.** This sounds elementary, but many company bonus plans are not as focused on the key metrics as they need to be. Look at the plan that is in place at your company. Are there ways for managers and employees to earn generous bonuses and/or stock options without making company sales and profit goals? If so, consider tightening up the plan so that there is a more direct correlation between payouts and company metrics.

CHAPTER 9

GO ON THE OFFENSE WHEN OTHERS RETRENCH

Vivek Paul's Bold Strategic Moves

This is only a transition. This is the time to invest and get your people in place so that when you return to normal times, you are well positioned to enjoy the benefits.

—VIVEK PAUL, CEO, Wipro Technologies

The true test of an organization's skill at creating effective leaders lies not in its ability to create what Peter Drucker calls CEO "geniuses or supermen." Rather, it lies in the organization's ability to consistently and systematically develop strong managers at all levels of the hierarchy. An organization that has a strong senior management team but lacks bench strength will find itself in trouble sooner rather than later—particularly when it comes to execution.

Jack Welch understood this as well as anyone. The GE operating system ensured a steady supply of capable leaders. Welch liked to say that GE's best products were not its aircraft engines or its medical devices, but its people. He thought more about the topic of leadership than almost any of his contemporaries, and this helped him to create a leadership cadre with both strong skill sets and an affinity for change.

This chapter is devoted to a former GE executive who never reported directly to Welch. Vivek Paul, an Indian national, was a senior executive in GE Medical in the 1990s. A generation "removed" from Welch, he reported instead to Jeff Immelt, who at the time headed GE's $8 billion medical systems division. Like his GE boss, Paul was a faithful follower of the company's predominant "religion," Six Sigma.

Welch loved the medical systems business because it typified GE's strengths in technology and innovation. When asked in the mid-1980s how he could sell off seemingly sacrosanct pieces of the company, such as the venerable housewares division, he asked rhetorically: "In the year 2000, would you rather be in toasters or CT scanners?" The choice of scanners to round out the contrast proved prescient: In subsequent years, Vivek Paul helped GE grab an astronomical *70 percent* of the U.S. CT (computerized tomography) scanner business.

Most American businesspeople have never heard of Paul. (This may be changing: At the end of 2004, *Time* named him—along with Jeff Immelt—one of the world's most influential businesspeople.) Despite his relatively low profile, however, he is a virtual poster boy for the GE leadership factory. As the head of GE's global CT Division, Paul spearheaded a revolutionary application of Six Sigma design called "four-slice CT" that led to GE's ability to leapfrog the competition and stay at least one year ahead of its closest rival.

Paul also drove up profit margins and sparked the productivity of the entire CT product line in markets as far away as France, Japan, and China. Finally, Paul also was president and CEO of GE's medical equipment joint venture in India, which has been heralded as one of the best-run joint ventures in GE's vast portfolio.

Given those achievements, it is not hard to imagine why Immelt did everything he could to keep Vivek Paul within the GE fold. It proved an impossible task. Azim Premji, chairman of an Indian conglomerate called Wipro, got hold of Paul and offered him command of the company's $150 million software division, Wipro Technologies. "You can build another skyscraper in New York," Premji told Paul, "or you can build a completely new thing in India." For an ambitious executive like Paul, the challenge was irresistible.

Face Reality and Instill Confidence

Paul spent his first three months at the company meeting with customers and employees. Despite the fact that he joined Wipro during the height of the dot-com boom, it soon became clear that the company faced several serious hurdles. According to one management insider, the psyches of Wipro employees was so fragile that most of them were convinced that they worked there only because they were not good enough to get a job elsewhere.

Without a doubt, the company's confidence problems were holding it back. Paul therefore vowed to come up with a plan that would make them proud to work at Wipro.

At the conclusion of his first 100 days on the job, he sent his employees a candid communiqué. (By so doing, he was living up to Welch's first law of business: *Force the organization to face reality.*) He told them that despite the current IT boom, Wipro could not compete in the long term if it remained on its current path. The company had to change if it was to compete.

As part of his effort to instill confidence into the psyche of the organization, he set a spectacular stretch goal, which he dubbed "4 x 4." His vision for Wipro, he announced, was to become a *$4 billion* business by 2004. (His starting point, remember, was a $150 million revenue base!) Although Wipro ultimately missed that goal by a significant margin, the audacious stretch goal nevertheless helped employees to believe in themselves and in the firm, whose revenues increased by 500 percent within five years. Welch, who decreed that "decimal points are a bore," would have approved of Paul's daring goal setting. What Wipro has done is

> *Go after initiative after initiative, building a wall*
> *of success that gives more and more traction.*

In addition to raising the growth bar higher than anyone thought possible, Paul made several strategic shifts that helped the company succeed. Like his counterparts at IBM, for example, he

FACE REALITY AND USE STRETCH GOALS TO MOTIVATE AND INSPIRE

After his first 100 days on the job, Vivek Paul let everyone know his candid assessment of the company. He later set an incredibly ambitious growth goal of $4 billion by 2004. Although the company missed this target by a wide margin, *setting the goal* was critically important in helping to instill confidence into the psyches of all who worked there. Facing reality and setting stretch goals are not inconsistent; rather, in tandem, they can play pivotal roles in forging a performance-based culture.

concluded that Wipro's future lay not in bidding for one-off, one-at-a-time projects but in providing integrated "end-to-end solutions." And even as the global recession at the turn of the century came on, hitting high-tech companies with special force, Paul increased spending selectively, trying to build new capacities in the company (discussed later in the chapter).

Spending while others were pulling back was a counterintuitive move that drew a lot of attention, but that was only a small piece of a much larger strategy. As he reinvented the business, Paul took a number of bold strategic steps that sealed Wipro's success and positioned it for strong growth for the future. And, as in most turnaround tales, the real story of Vivek Paul's transformation of Wipro can be discerned only in the details.

Transformation *Is* the Strategy

Since 1999, Paul has been vice chairman of Wipro and CEO of Wipro's Global Information Technology, Product Engineering, and Business Process Services segments. But these are relatively new areas for the Bangalore-based firm. The history of the company is, in fact, a *transformation* story driven by what the *Economist* calls "successful opportunistic diversification." Founded in 1945 as a vegetable oil company, it later morphed into a technology company, selling everything from light bulbs and printers to scanners and computers. The most recent part of the transformation has been to turn "cerebral," engaging in what one industry leader calls "brain arbitrage."

Peter Drucker probably would give Paul high marks for what he has achieved. That's because in charting the company's future, Paul has been putting into practice a key Drucker imperative articulated decades earlier. Long before it became fashionable to talk of "knowledge-based organizations," Drucker made a vital connection that, like so many of his other predictions, proved to be prescient:

> *Knowledge is the business fully as much as the customer is the business. . . . For business success, knowledge must first be meaningful to the customer in terms of satisfaction and value. Knowledge per se is useless in business (and not only in business); it is only effective through the contribution it makes outside of the business— to customers, markets and end-users.*

Vivek Paul understands that linkage between knowledge and customers. He has made Wipro India's premier software services corporation, a "global back-office for hire." His ultimate goal is to turn Wipro into a high-powered consulting firm that competes successfully with companies like Accenture, EDS, and IBM Global Consulting.

He is still a long way from competing head-to-head with the likes of IBM Global Consulting. But with a market capitalization in excess of $15 billion, the Wipro of 2005 competes successfully with many global technology heavyweights. It has won lucrative contracts from a wide range of companies—like Home Depot, Nokia, Delta Airlines, and Best Buy—in part because it has approached its markets flexibly:

> *We don't try to architect the perfect solution, we get our hands dirty, play with it as we change, adapt and grow. That's it.*

Since Paul took on the role of CEO of the services unit, the operating profits contributed to the larger Wipro organization by Paul's division have soared more than 35 percent annually.

But that dazzling number obscures an even more compelling story.

Paul's first years on the job were, in fact, rocky ones. Following the NASDAQ market meltdown of 2001, Wipro's rivals, such as Infosys, went into retrenching mode, slashing expenses and swearing off acquisitions for the foreseeable future. Paul himself conceded that the industry was entering the "danger zone."

Wipro's competitors decided that the best way to deal with the hangover brought on by the technology bubble was to hunker down, sit it out, and wait for better times. Vivek Paul could have done the same, thereby following the path of least resistance. Instead, he did exactly the opposite. He viewed the slowdown not as a time to retrench, but as a golden opportunity to go on the offensive:

> *I think you have to consider the slowdown in context. . . .*
> *The last year-and-a half saw a bubble form. It grew*
> *very fast and that was unsustainable. . . . We will*
> *continue to grow well after it. . . . Because we*
> *have a sound value equation. It involves taking*
> *great technological breadth and quality and process*
> *that is the world's best and offering it*
> *cost competitively.*

In the face of declining growth and profit margins, Paul increased the sales and marketing budget by almost 50 percent, and over the next two years he tripled the marketing and sales staffs. He also shelled out about $150 million to acquire companies in outsourcing and consulting. Collectively, it was a huge gamble, since there was no way to know how long it would take for the tech bust to run its course.

PRACTICE "OPPORTUNISTIC DIVERSIFICATION"

In today's superheated competitive marketplace, you must exploit whatever opportunities the marketplace offers. Paul saw a chance to better position his company for growth, even amidst the industry wreckage, and did not hesitate to go after it aggressively. Be proactive by constantly scanning the marketplace for new opportunities in your industry and key target markets.

Paul calls himself "inherently optimistic." Perhaps that was the deciding factor in his decision to execute such a bold agenda. Logically, one would *have* to be an optimist to go against the conventional business wisdom to the extent that he did. Here is how he put it in mid-2001, during the worst part of the tech recession:

> *There is much opportunity out there. This is only a transition. This is the time to invest and get your people in place so that when you return to normal times, you are well positioned to enjoy the benefits. . . . you may want the dust to settle, but if you wait and do nothing until then, you will probably fall behind the curve.*

Think Long-Term

Paul's strategy was not a wave of the magic wand, with immediate and positive results. In fact, implementing that strategy took a heavy toll in the near term. Following a great year in 2000 (63 percent top-line growth), growth slowed to the middle to upper

20 percent area in 2001 and 2002. Operating margins also fell by about a third. According to all these metrics, Wipro compared unfavorably with its competitors.

But ambitious strategies often take time to bear fruit. By 2004, Wipro was a $1.3 billion company and India's largest IT services corporation. Revenues once again grew by a stunning 60 percent over the previous year, and the stock price doubled in less than a year. Wipro also became the world's largest provider of out-sourced technology R&D, which aided its efforts in attracting customers in new sectors, such as the electronics and car industries.

Vivek Paul says that there are great opportunities for firms that understand the ever-changing dynamics of the information technology business. He thinks that when it comes to service, most American businesses remain relatively unenlightened. Managers and entrepreneurs don't understand the price-to-service-quality formula, contends Paul, which explains why so many U.S. companies are outsourcing to India. As evidence of this, tech guru Eric Lundquist recounts a story in which Paul took his nine-year-old car to an American service station.

Even after taking into account the face value of the coupons he had brought with him, he was told that repairs to his car would cost $92 per hour. Paul was shocked: "For 30 percent less than that," he later commented, "I can get engineers who can design a brand new car rather than fix this old one." Paul sees the rate of change accelerating and the winners being those that are capable of staying ahead of the curve:

> *We are moving to a world where everything has technology. I can't buy a car that doesn't have many, many electronics in it. My briefcase is going to be smart.*

*My house is going to be smart. If I don't have the ability
to service all these electronics in a way that is cost
competitive, there is no progress.*

Wipro is a company that "gets it." It has garnered numerous citations for its breakthrough process-quality methods and was declared one of the top 10 service providers and one of the best companies for leaders. The company went public in 2000, and in 2004, Paul—along with the CEOs of 3M, Apple, Intel, and Starbucks—was named one of the best managers in the world by *BusinessWeek*. He also was on the list of Silicon.com's 2004 "Agenda Setter List"—notably, one notch ahead of the CEO of the bluest of blue chips, IBM!

What explains Paul's success? His GE background and training are obviously key factors. Paul says that he learned much from his GE bosses, including "discipline in thinking." From Jeff Immelt, he learned "how you hide your raw talent . . . never overstate yourself." Humility is an important part of GE's authentic leadership model, and it is clearly implied in the 4E's.

It was also at GE that he learned about building a high-octane, performance-based culture, learned about stretch goals, and came to understand the importance of building an organization around shared values. He is a talented 4E Leader who has shown that he can execute consistently and make adjustments when necessary:

*You go down a path and every single day you look
around and ask yourself how you can do better,
and what twists and turns you need to take. If
you need to take the turn, take it without hesitation,
and never look back. It's about successfully making
the right decision versus some grand strategy.*

THINK INTEGRATED SOLUTIONS

Paul's prediction of a world full of smart machines, cars, and houses is almost upon us. He understands that only those companies that can serve customers' needs cost-efficiently will have a chance. But to garner long-term, consistent success, firms also will have to have the knowledge and competencies to satisfy a wide range of service needs. The companies that figure out how to satisfy several customer needs simultaneously will be the most competitive.

This and other comments by Paul show unmistakable traces of Welchian influence. In Welch's first major speech to stock analysts in 1981, the newly minted CEO told them that he had no "grand strategy" for GE. Quoting Prussian General Karl von Clausewitz, Welch made the point that most battle plans do not survive the first moments of conflict. Paul made more or less the same point more than two decades later.

Vivek Paul now leads a company with more than 30,000 employees in 24 locations around the world. In naming Paul one of the world's best managers, *Business Week* credited Paul's success to his "growth by acquisition" strategy. But there is much more to Wipro than acquisitions. There is also skilled *execution*. Here, Welch himself gives his opinion of Vivek Paul's company:

> *From the first day in dealing with Wipro, there's been nothing but quality, character, highest integrity, highest quality work. As a joint venture, you wouldn't find a better partner. As a supplier, you wouldn't find a higher quality partner.*

Create $100 Million Businesses

Paul's self-proclaimed goal was to turn Wipro into a "tech power-house." At the heart of his strategy was exploiting new opportunities by creating new competencies and new businesses. Within one four-year period ending in 2004, three new businesses accounted for 30 percent of the company's revenue and kept the company on its steep growth curve:

> *We answered the question of how would you have met the rising demand of services around the rising installed base of technology. We were in a situation where technology could have hit a bottleneck, but we learned to tap reservoirs of skills around the world.*

One opportunity Vivek saw was in enterprise applications. Rivals like Infosys were better positioned to win enterprise business when Paul took over. From 2000 to 2004, Paul focused on strengthening Wipro's enterprise applications business. In 2000, "package implementation" (PI) was only a $7 million business. But the tech swoon created new opportunities, as companies that had purchased pricey software systems sought help in maximizing their tech investments.

While elite U.S. consulting firms charged upwards of $130 per hour, Indian companies offered similar services for half that. That is why so many firms turned to India for help. In 1999, Wipro created a separate unit for enterprise applications services. By 2004, it was a $100 million-plus business that showed no signs of slowing down:

> *What has happened . . . over the last few years, what started with IT and is now spreading to engineering is an increasing ability to unlock potential around the world. To unlock capacity around the world.*

One other area that Paul set his sights on was "infrastructure management," which by 2004 was growing by 50 percent annually. Wipro had a domestic business in this area in 2000, but Paul took another page from the GE playbook by globalizing the business in 2001. By 2004, Wipro had almost three dozen large customers, including such enterprises as Best Buy and Lehman Brothers.

The biggest game-changer of all, however, was business process outsourcing (BPO). The company leapfrogged its rivals in the summer of 2002 when it acquired outsourcing firm Spectramind for $100 million. Critics were quick and sharp in their criticisms of the acquisition, with most of them concluding that Wipro had overpaid for the property.

Paul, however, held his ground. "We'll get more than we paid," he countered, "[and] that's the acid test of any investment." Many of the same critics later admitted that the acquisition had turned out to be a shrewd strategic move. By 2004, a scant two years later, the $100 million investment was valued at *seven times* what Wipro paid for it.

One of the keys to the company's ability to win big outsourcing contracts abroad is its ability to "localize senior management teams abroad." By doing this, Wipro is able to "take over the employee populations," which is something that would have been extremely difficult to achieve in the typical command-and-control organization of the past.

Despite its success in breaking down geographic boundaries, Paul knows that the company still has a long way to go. As a 4E Leader, Paul understands the importance of facing reality. It is also clear that Paul does not believe his own press clippings:

BECOME AN AUTHENTIC GLOBAL COMPANY

Paul said that his firm is not yet a global company but instead a company that sells its products globally. To be truly global, firms need to have an operational presence in international markets and to have locals run the businesses. Think global, but manage and train locally.

I think of ourselves as a global company, but I also know that's more of an ambition than a reality. Right now we are a company from India selling to customers everywhere in the world. I also don't want to get ahead of myself, but it's clear that we have to be a global company . . . but we're not there yet.

The 4E Leader To-Do List

☐ **Reassess value equations at regular intervals.** Organizations that deliver sound value equations—high-quality, competitively priced products and solutions—are better equipped to weather downturns and are far more likely to experience healthy growth when market conditions improve. Review your offerings (and your competitors' offerings) at least once a year to make sure that your value equations remain formidable. Weed out or enhance those products or services that require it.

☐ **Make strategic acquisitions in high-growth markets.** As Welch liked to say, "Business is not rocket science." Acquire companies that have the potential to enhance the organization's core competencies and market share in growth markets. Only a few years after Wipro bought Spectramind, despite the dire predictions, the company became one of Wipro's primary growth engines.

☐ **Convert knowledge into information that can be acted upon by customers.** In addition to equating knowledge and the customer ("Knowledge is the business"), Drucker added, "Physical goods or services are only the vehicle for the exchange of customer purchasing-power against business knowledge."

HOW TO USE THIS BOOK IN TRAINING, MANAGEMENT WORKSHOPS, AND PERFORMANCE REVIEWS

As discussed in Chapter 2, some of the best training that goes on in organizations takes place outside the classroom, in informal discussions, team meetings, and one-on-one coaching sessions. The most proactive managers know this intuitively. They ensure that their people have access to the information, tools, and training that they need to perform their jobs more effectively.

As an author, publisher, and editor, I have long been a big believer in using books as learning tools. Books are low-tech and inexpensive, and when used properly, they have the capacity to provoke thought while helping to change the mind-set of an individual or group. Reading a book prior to a more structured training session can set the stage for meaningful discussion and additional learning.

There are several ways that a manager can put this book to work in his or her organization. Here are a few ideas:

■ *Give a copy of the book to everyone on your team or in your unit or division.* It need not be more complex than that. Almost everyone loves books, and you can be assured that this book will be well received if you hand it out with a personal (preferably handwritten) note of encouragement.

Including a note is an important step. That's because in some instances involving more sensitive individuals, receiving a business "how-to" book from a boss may be misinterpreted as a gesture of criticism. For example, someone who receives this book may think that his or her boss is "trying to tell him or her something."

Conversely, a positive note of support and a simple handwritten "*Thank you for the great work*" can do wonders in motivating an individual or team. Welch was the master of the handwritten note, sending them often to key GE leaders, praising them for everything from achieving great results with Six Sigma to improving inventory turns and operating margins.

If you do give out copies to your team, you may want to schedule a brown-bag or pizza lunch to discuss it. This kind of informal gathering is conducive to a candid and thoughtful discussion and has the potential to get the most reticent employees involved.

■ *Incorporate the book into a formal training session.* In this instance, it is best to get copies of the book to the team at least two or three weeks before the meeting. Once again, handing out the books with a personal note can help secure buy-in to the event.

The 4E model will give you and your team plenty of opportunities to share stories in which having one or more of the E's made a real difference in closing a sale, making a key acquisition, or retaining and promoting a key member of the unit.

It also will prove to be a very useful tool in discussing some of the tougher issues facing a management team, such as poor performers, poor execution, lack of drive, and so on. What follows are minicases in which the book can be used as the focal point of a training session, a management workshop, or an executive summit.

How to Use This Book in Management Training

There are many ways in which this book can be used as a training tool. How one chooses to use the book will differ from organization to organization and from group to group depending on the specific goals of the management training, as well as the skills and competencies of the members of the unit.

What follows are three very specific scenarios in which a manager can use the book to achieve different results. They were written as case examples in the hope that you and other leaders would find some similarities to your own organizations in the situations that are given. The three examples given will show a leader how to use the book:

1. To *transform* an organization

2. To *inspire* and *motivate*

3. As a core concept in *performance reviews*

SCENARIO 1: TO *TRANSFORM* AN ORGANIZATION

In the seat of the CEO: In this scenario, let's assume that you are a middle manager in a medium-sized manufacturing company. Your firm has just acquired a rival, one that has been struggling for years. No matter what they tried, previous management could not manage to turn things around and meet their sales or profit goals—not once in the previous seven quarters.

Upon making the $50 million acquisition, your company promotes you to senior vice president and puts you in charge of the newly acquired unit. With the exception of the CEO, COO, and CFO, all other management is still in place.

After working with the organization's managers for three months, you realize that the company has a terrible confidence problem. Evidently, the former CEO was a micromanager without peer. There were so many layers of red tape that almost nothing got done. All of this is killing morale, which in part explains why the company had been floundering for so long.

Your job is to instill confidence into the company and to get managers (and employees) to think and act on their own. Until they do, you realize, this will always be a second-rate unit. You set your sights on transforming the company's entrenched culture of hesitation and procrastination.

You sense fear throughout the organization. They fear everything, from making the wrong decision to making *any* decision at all. If all this was not bad enough, the company's organization chart makes no sense, only adding bureaucracy to its woes. There are nine management layers between the shop floor and the

CEO, despite the company's relatively modest size (revenues will be down again this year, to under $90 million).

The departed CEO ran an antiquated command-and-control organization that was as regimented as any army or navy unit. No one seemed to want to be there (*the unit had few energizers*). Middle managers and employees in your unit were "punished" for failure, resulting in a staff that was terrified of making the wrong call (translation: *no edge*). Finally, the division has become accustomed to—no, worse, *comfortable with*—missing its key budget goals (*poor execution*). It is clear that the culture of the company in no way resembles that of a performance-based organization.

In addition, senior managers have not shared information with employees, so while almost everyone knows that the company has been doing poorly, most don't understand why or what metrics need to be improved to turn things around (e.g., operating margins).

You decide to host a two-day off-site meeting with the 12 senior managers who have been retained after the acquisition. This is your management team (for better or worse) because all report directly to you.

In the past 90 days, you have gotten to know a good deal about this group, and you sense that there is plenty of "runway" there. Despite the shortcomings in some of their management styles (like their CEO, few understand the importance of delegation), you sense that there is a strong management team dying to break out.

They are a smart bunch; they really understand the intricacies of their business, and they want to succeed. The problem is that they have been led poorly, and they need to break from the past. You see the 4E model, at least in part, as something of an antidote to the division's ills.

You decide that the best course of action is to let them all know what you expect of them, to draw a vivid picture of the "finish line" (a performance-based firm with winning in its blood), and to give each of them six months to demonstrate that he or she can perform at the high level that you have described.

To launch things in proper fashion, you send each manager a copy of this book with a warm note of encouragement. You ask each of them to read the book in preparation for the off-site meeting. You also send an agenda along with the book and handwritten note.

The morning sessions are analytical in nature. They set the stage for a frank discussion and send a strong message: From this day on, you are committed to developing a performance-based culture, one in which the quality of their ideas will be a key measure of their contributions.

You also plan to tell them that you will not tolerate those who cannot live with the changes you are making or those who cannot step up to the plate and deliver the results that the organization requires them to deliver to turn the company around.

You expect managers to lead—not by pulling rank or with intimidation tactics, but by the strength of their vision and their commitment to continuous improvement. You expect your managers to make the tough decisions (*edge:* who to hire, fire, and promote), and you also expect them to deliver strong results (*execute*).

Here, for illustrative purposes, is a model agenda that might prove helpful when putting together your *own* program. It is intended only as an example. Any leader worth his or her salt should go to great lengths to tailor an agenda to the particular needs of the management team and organization.

218

SAMPLE AGENDA, NOVEMBER 14, OFF-SITE MEETING: BECOMING A "4E LEADER"

8:00–8:30: *Opening remarks: Defining The 4E Leader: energy, energize, edge,* and *execute*

8:30–9:00: *The significance of the 4E Leadership model* (how it was used at GE)

9:00–10:00: *Hiring for the E's* (how to spot a 4E Leader)

10:00–11:00: *Training and promoting the E's* (creating a performance-based culture)

11:00–12:00: *Identifying the next layer of leaders using the 4E model*

12:00–1:00: *Working lunch.* Looking in the mirror exercise—an honest assessment of our senior management "E-profile"

The afternoon sessions are devoted to increasing the "E-quotient" of the entire team and, in turn, the entire organization. These sessions are more application oriented, intended to drill down to the specific acts and initiatives that will move the performance "needle" (i.e., make a real difference).

Afternoon discussions:

1:00–2:00: Ways to instill *energy* throughout the organization

2:00–3:00: How to *energize* troops (what's the vision?)

3:00–4:00: Infusing *edge* throughout the organization

4:00–5:00: Developing a culture for *execution*

This is obviously an extreme example of a company that is in dire need of help. However, almost every organization faces some of these same challenges. For example, even the most progressive, forward-thinking organizations have some red tape and bureaucracy. In addition, many companies have autocratic managers who lead by command and control rather than with the strength of their vision.

SCENARIO 2: TO *INSPIRE* AND *MOTIVATE*

In the seat of the CEO: In this scenario, you are a franchise owner of a $5 million business. There are a total of nine managers in the firm and a total of 40 employees. Your unit has just come off the best year in its 10-year history. Despite the fact that the economy grew by less than 3 percent, your business achieved year-over-year growth in excess of 15 percent!

Delighted with the efforts of the entire unit, you decide to hold your next managers' meeting in Scottsdale, Arizona. You want to thank your management team for their achievements. But that's not the only reason you decide to take them to the warm environs of Arizona.

Your team, simply put, is burned out. That double-digit growth they racked up came with a price. All your managers had to put in 15-hour days, six days a week for the last two months in order to exceed their budget and profit goals. The Scottsdale trip will give them a chance to get some rest, check out the great golf courses, and "recharge their batteries" for the upcoming year.

You schedule a five-day meeting that includes one full day of tennis and golf and four half-day morning meetings. The theme of the meeting is "*Second to None: Taking Our Business to the Next Level.*"

You select this theme for several reasons: First, you want to praise the team for their great efforts. None of your rivals came close to achieving 15 percent growth, and you want them all to know that they have your confidence.

In your opening remarks, you also make it clear that this is not the time to rest on their laurels or become complacent. Since you are the market leader, all your competitors will be gunning for you in the year ahead. Since this will be the first time that your firm has had a proverbial "bulls eye on its back," it is incumbent upon the group to get even better (one of the books written about Welch was called *Get Better or Get Beaten*).

In addition to establishing this positive theme, you sketch out your vision for the meeting: The goal, you tell your small team, is to provide them with the ideas, tools, and leadership models that will help them take the company to the next level.

You explain that despite the company's recent phenomenal success, "We don't have all the answers." Our goal then, is to do the following:

Master the ideas and concepts that will help us to maintain the edge we have worked so hard to establish. We will now—and forever—seek continuous improvement, and the only real way to do that is to make learning our company's most precious currency that will enrich us both personally and professionally as we take our company to the next level.

The meeting agenda for the four days ahead includes several leadership ideas and models, each to be the primary focus of one of the four morning sessions. You decide to kick off day one with the 4E model, since you view that as one of the seminal ideas that will assist your managers to become better motivators. (That's important, since you perceive that to be one of the team's few weaknesses.)

A half-day session as outlined here could be a great way to motivate a team that has performed well while simultaneously getting the group to think through new ways to hire and promote and to make key decisions more quickly.

Of course, there are other ways to use the book to inspire a team, and there are many other ways to structure an agenda. (Interestingly enough, Welch preferred to operate without a

---

SAMPLE AGENDA, NOVEMBER 14, OFF-SITE MEETING:

SECOND TO NONE:
TAKING OUR COMPANY TO THE NEXT LEVEL

8:00–8:30: *Opening remarks: "A Great Year in Review"* (*Execution*)

8:30–9:00: *The 4E Leadership model:* How it will make us even more competitive in the year ahead

9:00–10:00: *Raising the bar:* How to hire and promote on the 4E's

10:00–11:00: *Maintaining our edge:* Making the tough decisions faster and better

11:00–12:00: *Energize and execute:* How to create a performance-based culture

12:00–1:00 *Working lunch:* Brainstorming session: other ways to apply the 4E model to our firm (e.g., in performance reviews)

---

detailed agenda, preferring to lay out an item or two and let things flow from there.) Regardless of the agenda, however, the key is getting the book into the hands of your key people and engaging them in a meaningful discussion about the E's and how they can help spur new ideas, growth, and productivity.

SCENARIO 3: HOW TO USE THE E'S IN *PERFORMANCE REVIEWS*

The E's are also a powerful tool that you and your firm can use at annual review time and at any time in between. Understandably, many managers, especially those who have weak performers on their team, hate writing and delivering performance reviews. After all, how many people actually look forward to telling people that their work is not cutting it?

As discussed in Chapter 2, the most effective managers engage their people in meaningful discussions all year round. This way, your direct reports have a pretty clear idea of where they stand long before their annual review.

The 4E model is a useful construct at annual review time, and it also can help in those informal discussions managers have with their people all the time. One of the benefits of the 4E Leadership model is that it allows the manager to describe an archetypal figure—a leadership ideal.

By painting a vivid picture of The 4E Leader early on, the manager can, at the outset, establish some fundamental expectations regarding performance. When a manager tells his or her team that the 4E's are the "price of admission," he or she is sending a very powerful message: *I am raising the bar. I expect each of you to have energy and passion, spark others to perform, make difficult choices, and consistently execute and exceed your goals.*

One other advantage of the 4E model is that it allows for an objective, qualitative metric that can help a manager offer a complete assessment of an employee. It can be used as a useful tool that can supplement an organization's existing review measurements, especially quantitative criteria. Let's take a few examples.

In the seat of the CEO: In this scenario, a vice president of sales has a district sales manager who has missed his sales quota two out of the last three years. Before joining the management team, Dave was one of the firm's most successful salespeople, blowing away his numbers year after year. Now, after yet another year of disappointing results, he is in something of a state of shock. He has never failed before, and he can't get his hands around what he is doing wrong.

In addition to managing eight salespeople, Dave still maintains half a dozen key accounts, and they are faring better than ever: Sales are up 40 percent this year. Why, then, are six of the eight other salespeople treading water at best?

One of the obvious answers is that being a great salesperson does not necessarily translate into being a great sales *manager.* The numbers tell Dave that he is performing poorly; they don't, however, tell him *why.* That's where The 4E Leadership model can help.

After talking directly to some of the manager's salespeople (with the manager's encouragement), you get the impression that this manager is still doing what he did best: sell! Dave is intensely focused on his *own* accounts, since that's what he knows how to do. He is simply not spending enough time with his people, and as a result, his sales staff feels isolated, unappreciated, and unfocused.

When he does spend time with his salespeople, he is rather harsh with his criticism, which puts a damper on both morale and confidence. He seems to have little patience with salespeople who don't close quickly enough (he is a quick closer). In other words, Dave is a poor *energizer*. He does not lead with a vision or spark others to perform; instead, although he does not mean to, he spreads pessimism and negativity.

In giving your review of this district manager, you go through the numbers and give your district manager a chance to respond: "I know my district numbers aren't great, but aren't I setting the right example by hitting the ball out of the park with my own accounts?" he pleads.

"Your accounts are doing great," you counter, "but that doesn't help your salespeople manage *their* accounts." You ask the manager how much time he is spending with his direct reports, and you also ask him to describe a typical day in the field with one of his salespeople. In answering, he stammers his way through a long-winded, defensive response. It is clear that he is feeling that he is being "attacked" and unfairly judged. That's when you shift gears.

You take a step back and start talking about your expectations for all managers. You then describe the archetypal 4E Leader. You tell him something like this: "Dave, salespeople who are rich in the 4E's are the best performers. That's because they have great energy, articulate a vision for how their products or services solve customer problems, know when to walk away from a negotiation, and almost always make their numbers."

It's clear that your sales manager now *gets it*. With your urging, he then assesses each of his direct reports and how they stack up against the 4E ideal: "Salesperson X," he reports, "has energy and the ability to energize but can never say no. He promises more than he can deliver (no edge). That's why his execution has been poor." "Salesperson Y," he continues, "lacks enthusiasm; she has no energy or urgency. That's why she misses her numbers."

After about a half hour of this, you decide to turn the tables: "OK, Dave, let's talk about you. Where do *you* come out on the E's?" Dave stops for a moment and then begins to smile. By explaining the concept and then asking him to rate his people against the 4E model, you have achieved something important: You have gotten him off the defensive.

Now when he is asked to look inside himself, he is in a better frame of mind to evaluate his own strengths and weaknesses. That's because he now doesn't see it as "me against the world" or "senior management against me"; instead, he sees the constructive aspects of rating himself against an objective benchmark. After all, if measuring his own people against the 4E model proved to be a fruitful exercise, why would it be less so for their manager?

After a more detailed discussion, you learn that he has actually been avoiding his team. Perhaps not consciously, but he has. Upon digging further, you learn the reason: He has no confidence in his ability to lead others. Dave has always considered himself a great salesperson, but deep down, he never really believed that he would make a great manager.

He has never had the chance to lead, having always been a follower. That's why he considers himself something of a charlatan for having been promoted to district manager. But what could he do? Turn down the promotion? It didn't seem like an option at the time. Besides, he could use the extra money, and he did not want to ponder the loss of face he would surely endure when word spread like wildfire that he was not up for the new position.

Dave opens up to you: He knows that he has *energy* and *edge* . . . but he concludes that he has a difficult time *energizing* his people. You thank him for his honesty, and then you vow to work with him to improve his capabilities in this area. Now that the problem is out in the open, at least you know where to start.

You pair him up with a mentor, a fellow district manager with more than two decades of experience and a record of great leadership. You also promise to allocate more of your time to coaching him so that he can, in turn, become a better coach to his people.

A qualitative measurement like the 4E's works most effectively when it is used in conjunction with a quantitative measurement.

In this instance, the problem with the district manager surfaced when the numbers for his territory came in. The fact that three-quarters of the salespeople in that district failed to make their goals alerted you to a serious problem.

But, as mentioned earlier, the sales numbers served only as a warning flag. They did not tell you *what* the problem was or *why* Dave was failing as a sales manager. A qualitative measurement like the 4E's can help pinpoint specific *habits* and *behaviors* that are derailing a manager's performance.

And ultimately, as Peter Drucker pointed out more than five decades ago, management is all about doing. It's about performing tasks, managing managers, and creating a business that achieves its goals:

> *And yet the ultimate test of management is business performance. Achievement rather than knowledge remains,*

of necessity, both proof and aim. Management, in other words, is a practice, rather than a science or a profession, though containing elements of both.

As a manager of managers, your job is very clear: It is to help others achieve and perform. That's how organizations, of any size and in any industry, produce winning results.

ACKNOWLEDGMENTS

I would like to acknowledge the talented McGraw-Hill team that helped to make this book a reality. My editor, Philip Ruppel, made this a far richer work with his vision and publishing instincts. I would also like to thank Lynda Luppino, Eileen Lamadore, and Allyson Gonzalez for their extensive contributions, as well as Tom Lau, David Dell'Accio, Anthony Sarchiapone, and Dan Stivers for their creativity and attention to detail. Thanks also, to the great team in Asia: Joseph Chong, LeeKheng Teo, Gunawan Hadi, and Vitit Lim have helped all of us to "globalize the intellect" of our books and businesses.

Thanks also, to my tireless assistant, Laura Libretti, who never fails to make all the McGraw-Hill trains run on time. Thanks also, to Lydia Rinaldi, McGraw-Hill's indefatigable director of publicity, who with great perseverance, ensures that none of my books wither in obscurity. And finally, thanks to Daina Penikas and Maureen Harper, who turn ideas and pages into handsome volumes that inspire and educate.

I have long since believed that good works are built upon sturdy foundations laid by others. The remarkable Peter Drucker, the inventor of modern management, has lit the way for many a business writer for six decades. For their research, insights, and writings, thanks also to Peter Senge, Noel Tichy, Stratford Sherman, Jeffrey Immelt, Vivek Paul, James McNerney, Larry Bossidy, and Ram Charan.

And, of course, Jack Welch, who has been my subject of study for more than fifteen years. Welch is—to the *practice* of leadership—what Peter Drucker is to the *field* of management.

A heartfelt thank you, also, to the hard-charging Home Depot CEO, Robert Nardelli, for taking time to share his leadership thoughts and insights, which played a vital role in formulating many of the ideas in this book.

Jeffrey L. Cruikshank has once again brought his considerable talent to bear on another McGraw-Hill book. For his fine efforts I am truly grateful.

Thanks also, to my incredible wife Nancy and my two little packages of "E's," Noah and Joshua. All three inspire and energize, helping to remind me of what is truly important.

SOURCES AND NOTES

Below you will find the sources and notes regarding the researching of this book. Before I do that, I would like to cite several works that have been particularly helpful for this and other books I have written on the subject of leadership.

To begin with, any management/leadership author would be remiss without citing the works of Peter Drucker. His two ground-breaking works, *Concept of the Corporation* (1946) and *The Practice of Management* (1954), are and will remain two of the watershed books that established management as a social institution and distinct field of study. As the father of modern management (and the "Clairvoyant of Claremont," as I call him), he built the foundation on which so many leadership authors have relied to build their management and leadership models. Other important works include Noel Tichy and Stratford Sherman's *Control Your Destiny or Someone Else Will* (Doubleday Currency, 1993), the second book ever written on Mr. Welch and his management methods and one of the most comprehensive. Mr. Welch's own work, *Jack: Straight from the Gut* (Warner, 2001), provided some important details and anecdotes. Bossidy and Charan's best-selling work, *Execution* (Crown Business, 2002), also yielded several important ideas regarding the fourth E of leadership. Also, Peter Senge's 1994 work, *The Fifth Discipline Fieldbook* (Currency, 1994), was very helpful in developing some of the key points in Chapters 1 and 2.

Introduction

Welch's evaluation of the Democratic presidential candidates is given in *Wall Street Journal,* Jan. 23, 2004, p. A14.

In addition to establishing direction . . .: John Kotter, *A Force for Change* (New York: Free Press, 1990), p. 5.

"You have your stars . . .": Peter Drucker, *Managing in the Next Society,* (New York: St. Martin's Press), p. 90.

The statement concerning 25 percent of the largest Fortune 500 companies' CEOs comes from Larry Bossidy and Ram Charan, *Execution* (New York: Crown Business, 2002), p. 14.

"You're either the best at what you do . . .": 1983 GE Annual Report, quoted in Noel Tichy and Stratford Sherman and Stratford Sherman, *Control Your Own Destiny or Someone Else Will* (New York: Doubleday Currency, 1993, revised in 2001), p. 85.

"GE had been inside-out . . .": Brent Schlender, "The Odd Couple," *Fortune,* May 1, 2000, p. 126.

"By ending his career with failure . . .": T. R. Reid, *The United States of Europe* (Penguin: New York, 2004), pp. 105–106.

The idea that in Asia, Welch books topped best-seller lists is supported by the fact that *The Welch Way* (also by Jeffrey A. Krames), debuted at number 5 in Japan in early 2005.

"One can only build on strength. . . .": Peter Drucker, *The Practice of Management* (New York: HarperCollins, 1954), pp. 150–151.

Welch's beliefs concerning the qualities of leaders come from Noel Tichy and Stratford Sherman, *Control Your Own Destiny or Someone Else Will.*

"It is a wheel-spinning exercise . . .": Robert Slater, *Jack Welch on Leadership* (New York: McGraw-Hill, 2003), p. 17. It should be noted that this book was the abridged version of *Jack Welch and the GE Way* by the same author and publisher, 1997.

Chapter 1

Welch's discussion of passion comes from Jack Welch: *Jack: Straight from the Gut* (New York: Warner Books, 2001), p. 385.

"The higher up an executive . . .": Peter Drucker, *Effective Executive* (New York: HarperCollins, 1967), p. 49.

"I was afforded a tremendous amount of opportunities at GE . . .": Robert Nardelli interview with author's representative on Feb. 3, 2005. For the record, all of the questions posed to Mr. Nardelli were written by author (Jeffrey Krames) but conducted by author's representative due to a timing conflict. From this point on, this interview will be referred to as "interview with Robert Nardelli."

"Any time there is a change . . .": Ibid.

"A primary task in taking a company from good to great . . .": Jim Collins, *Good to Great* (New York: Harper Collins, 2001), p. 88.

"If you are not on fire about what you're doing . . .": Jeffrey Krames, *What the Best CEOs Know* (New York: McGraw-Hill, 2003).

"Leading from good to great . . .": Jim Collins, *Good to Great,* p. 75.

"Leadership is about creating a climate . . .": Jim Collins, *Good to Great,* p. 74.

"It seems so simple at first glance . . .": Susan Frank in Peter Senge, *The Fifth Discipline Fieldbook* (New York: Doubleday Currency, 1994), p. 223).

The discussions of the three architectural design elements come from Peter Senge, *The Fifth Discipline Fieldbook* (New York, Doubleday Currency, 1994), p. 36, 37.

Senge conclusion regarding the number of companies that embraced all three guiding ideas comes from Peter Senge, *The Fifth Discipline Fieldbook,* p. 38.

Chapter 2

"Big corporations are filled with people . . .": *Jack Welch and the GE Way* (New York: McGraw-Hill, 1998), pp. 114–115.

"Our strategy for the Home Depot...": interview with Robert Nardelli, Feb. 3, 2005.

"I may be kidding myself...": John Byrne, "How Jack Runs GE," *Business Week,* June 8, 1998, p. 98.

"Many organizations unintentionally encourage the reactive orientation . . .": Peter Senge, *The Fifth Discipline Fieldbook,* p. 227.

"This boundaryless learning culture . . .": Jack Welch speech at GE annual meeting, Charlotte, North Carolina, April 23, 1997.

"The quality of an idea does not depend on its altitude . . .": *Jack Welch and the GE Way,* p. 97; interview with Jack Welch, *Industry Week,* May 2, 1994.

"If you, I and the business leadership . . .": Jack Welch speech, the Bay Area Council, San Francisco, Sept. 6, 1997.

"I know if I pan this room . . .": Welch speech, 92nd Street Y, Q&A, March 8, 1999.

The discussion of social software and social operating systems can be found in Larry Bossidy and Ram Charan, *Execution*, p. 98–99.

The discussion of questions to be asked at review time comes from Peter Senge, *The Fifth Discipline Fieldbook*, p. 221. Please note that these are not verbatim citations but are paraphrased and amended by this author.

What Welch wanted to know in his discussions at Crotonville is covered in Jack Welch, *Jack: Straight from the Gut*, p. 177. The wording of the questions has been paraphrased.

"Without productivity growth . . .": Noel Tichy and Stratford Sherman, *Control Your Own Destiny or Someone Else Will*, p. 197.

". . . we've really tried to create . . .": interview with Robert Nardelli, Feb. 3, 2005.

"The deal changed the atmosphere": Jack Welch, *Jack: Straight from the Gut*, p. 144.

"One cannot do anything with what one cannot do. . . .": Peter Drucker, *The Practice of Management*, p. 151.

"My view of the 1990s . . .": Noel Tichy and Stratford Sherman, *Control Your Own Destiny or Someone Else Will*, pp. 203–204.

The idea of "selling runway" comes from Jack Welch, *Jack: Straight from the Gut*, p. 84.

"We have found that by reaching for what appears to be impossible . . .": Jack Welch speech, Charlottesville, Virginia, April 24, 1996.

Chapter 3

"The market is rewarding you like Super Bowl winners . . .": John A. Byrne, "How Jack Welch Runs GE," *BusinessWeek*, June 8, 1998, p. 99.

Giuliani's preparation for becoming mayor and the consequences of it come from Rudy Giuliani, *Leadership* (New York: Miramax Books, 2002), pp. 56–57.

He had to find a way of "managing long term . . .": Jack Welch, *Jack: Straight from the Gut*, p. 124.

The discussion of Welch's payroll cuts and facilities upgrades comes from Robert Slater, *The New GE* (New York: McGraw-Hill, 1992), and Jack Welch, *Jack: Straight from the Gut*, pp. 121–122.

"Paradox is a way of life. . . .": Noel Tichy and Stratford Sherman, *Control Your Own Destiny or Someone Else Will*, p. 143.

"Differentiation is all about being extreme . . .": Jack Welch, *Jack: Straight from the Gut*, p. 25.

"Just look at the way baseball teams pay . . .": Jack Welch, *Jack: Straight from the Gut*, p. 25.

The statement that GE lost less than 1 percent of its A's comes from Jack Welch, *Jack: Straight from the Gut*, p. 160.

The discussion of the need to rid the company of C's comes from Jack Welch, *Jack: Straight from the Gut*, p. 160.

"Who questions come before 'what' decisions . . .": Jim Collins, *Good to Great*, p. 63.

The discussion of the need to fact reality when making people decisions comes from Jim Collins, *Good to Great*, p. 63.

Chapter 4

The five questions that any manager should be able to answer come from Robert Slater, *The GE Way Fieldbook: Jack Welch's Battle Plan for Corporate Revolution*, (New York: McGraw-Hill, 2000), p. 24.

"It's great to think about the future . . .": Robert Slater, *The GE Way Fieldbook*, p. 26.

The discussion of the six areas in which the best leaders excelled (starting with "performance") comes from Robert Slater, *The GE Way Fieldbook*, pp. 27–29.

"I think it's the combination . . .": interview with Robert Nardelli, Feb. 3, 2005.

"We have to continually look outside ourselves . . .": ibid.

The elements that go into good execution are discussed in Larry Bossidy and Ram Charan, *Execution*, p. 6.

"Building houses with no foundations": Larry Bossidy and Ram Charan, *Execution*, p. 6.

"Execution is a systematic process . . .": Larry Bossidy and Ram Charan, *Execution*, p. 22.

The discussion of execution-oriented culture comes from Larry Bossidy and Ram Charan, *Execution*, p. 30.

The material on the $500 club comes from Jack Welch, *Jack: Straight from the Gut*, p. 35.

The list of causes of poor execution and possible remedies comes from Robert Slater, *The GE Way Fieldbook*, p. 31.

Part 2

Drucker's discussion of the importance of the management team comes from Peter Drucker, *The Practice of Management,* p. 111.

"Managers cannot create leaders. . . .": Peter Drucker, *The Practice of Management,* p. 159.

The material on CEO turnover and managers' lack of desire to be CEO comes from Del Jones, "You Want Me to Be Your CEO? No Way!" *USA Today,* Oct. 6, 2004.

Welch's praise of his three possible successors comes from Jack Welch, *Jack: Straight from the Gut,* p. 407.

Chapter 5

"Companies that seek to compete and grow . . .": Jeffrey Immelt, Hatfield Lecture, Cornell University, April 15, 2004.

"Jeff had taken our medical systems business . . .": Jack Welch, *Jack: Straight from the Gut,* pp. 419–420.

Immelt's decision regarding the insurance business comes from the letter to shareowners in the GE 2003 Annual Report.

"Immelt isn't buying growth . . .": Jerry Useem, *Fortune,* April 5, 2004, p. 118.

"Instead of announcing some half-baked turnaround scheme . . .": Jerry Useem, *Fortune,* April 5, 2004, p. 123.

The source for Immelt's discussion of "growth engines," "cash generators" and "five new realities" in this chapter is Jeffrey Immelt, 2003 letter to stakeholders, 2003 Annual Report. (note that Mr. Immelt changed the name of the letter from "shareowners" to "stakeholders").

"85 percent of the company . . .": Diane Brady, "Immelt's GE Looks Like a Marathoner," *BusinessWeek,* Dec. 24, 2003.

"Two important lessons . . .": 2003 Letter to Stakeholders, GE Annual Report, 2003.

"There is not one person in GE . . .": Diane Brady, "Will Jeff Immelt's Push Pay Off for GE?," *BusinessWeek,* Oct. 13, 2001, pp. 94–98.

"Growth is the initiative . . .": Jeffrey Immelt, 2003 Letter to Stakeholders, GE 2003 Annual Report.

Immelt's attitude toward the services segment comes from Jeffrey Immelt, 2002 GE annual meeting, Louisville, Kentucky, April 28, 2004.

Chapter 6

Leadership development is about getting people to grow . . .": "James McNerney, 3M CEO of the Year," *Industry Week*, Jan. 1, 2004.

"I've got to make it culturally okay to say no": Jerry Useem, "Can McNerney Reinvent 3M?" *Fortune*, Aug. 12, 2002.

The source for McNerney's five part productivity plan on p. 145 is William Miller, New Leader, New Era, *Industry Week*, Nov. 1, 2001.

McNerney's decision to drive change from the bottom up is discussed in Jerry Useem, "Can McNerney Reinvent 3M?" *Fortune*, Aug. 12, 2002.

McNerney's growth goal of 10 percent comes from Carol Hymowitz, "Winning the Support of the Rank and File," *Wall Street Journal*, April 24, 2002.

"In the old world . . .": "James McNerney, New World Leader James McNerney, CEO of the Year," *Industry Week*, Jan. 1, 2004.

"Some people think . . .": *Fortune*, April 12, 2004, p. 65.

"My experience is . . .": *Fortune*, April 12, 2004, p. 68.

"3M had a tendency . . .": Carol Hymowitz, "Winning the Support of the Rank and File," *Wall Street Journal*, April 24, 2002.

McNerney's focus on the 3M businesses with the greatest prospects for growth is discussed in Michael Arndt, "3M's Rising Star," *BusinessWeek*, April 12, 2004, p. 69.

"We know we can't manage the global economy . . .": James McNerney, 3M shareholders meeting, May 2001.

"Leadership development is about helping people grow . . .": James McNerney, "New World Leader James McNerney, CEO of the Year," *Industry Week*, Jan. 1, 2004.

"The same energy and entrepreneurism . . .": McNerney, Training Directors' Forum e-Net, July 3, 2002.

McNerney's recognition of the need for a single approach to quality is discussed in "New World Leader James McNerney, CEO of the Year," *Industry Week*, Jan. 1, 2004.

"Being more responsive to customers . . .": James McNerney, Training Directors' Forum e-Net, July 3, 2002.

The statement about promotion of employees trained in Six Sigma comes from Michael Arndt, "3M's Rising Star," *BusinessWeek*, April 12, 2004, p. 72.

The source for the sidebar on using Six Sigma to align improvement effort with business strategy and cultural transformation is James McNerney in summit with Dr. Joseph Juran, June 2002.

"I'm responsible for keeping 3M a globally competitive company . . .": Michael Arndt, "3M's Rising Star," *BusinessWeek,* April 12, 2004, p. 72.

The 3M tradition of "sideways technology" comes from Training Directors' Forum e-Net, July 3, 2002.

McNerney's 2x/3x plan is discussed in American Productivity & Quality Center, *Using Knowledge Management to Drive Innovation* (APQC Press, 2003).

3M's investment in R&D is given in Michael Arndt, "3M's Rising Star," *BusinessWeek,* April 12, 2004, p. 64.

"The best and most sustainable innovation . . . .": James McNerney, In Good Company Web site, Leaders.

"I think we're world-class at the front end . . .": Jerry Useem, "Can McNerney Reinvent GE?" *Fortune,* Aug. 12, 2002.

The 15 percent time policy is discussed in "McNerney '71 Talks Leadership," *Yale Daily News,* Feb. 13, 2004.

"3M values individual ideas . . .": "McNerney '71 Talks Leadership," *Yale Daily News,* Feb. 13, 2004.

"The adhesives in Post-its . . .": "McNerney '71 Talks Leadership," *Yale Daily News,* Feb. 13, 2004.

Chapter 7

"I get more satisfaction from seeing things get done than I do about philosophizing or building sand castles . . .": Larry Bossidy, Q&A, *Time,* July 1, 2002.

"Execution is not just tactics. . . .": Larry Bossidy, "Execution as Attitude," *The Chief Executive,* May 2002.

Welch's initial excitement with Bossidy is told in Jack Welch, *Jack: Straight from the Gut,* p. 73. His later regard for Bossidy is mentioned on p. 95 of the same book.

"The challenge of the new Crotonville team . . .": Noel Tichy and Stratford Sherman, *Control Your Own Destiny or Someone Else Will,* p. 132.

Bossidy's handling of the Crotonville class and his response to the job security question are from Noel Tichy and Stratford Sherman, *Control Your Own Destiny or Someone Else Will,* p. 136.

Tichy's description of Bossidy as "an instinctive populist" comes from Noel Tichy and Stratford Sherman, *Control Your Own Destiny or Someone Else Will,* p. 140.

GE's hosting management workshops at distant destinations is discussed in Noel Tichy and Stratford Sherman, *Control Your Own Destiny or Someone Else Will,* p. 140.

Welch's getting rid of GE's strategic planning staff is covered in Noel Tichy and
    Stratford Sherman, *Control Your Own Destiny or Someone Else Will,* p. 140.
"A separate planning function . . .": Noel Tichy and Stratford Sherman,
    Control Your Own Destiny or Someone Else Will, p. 281; Bossidy presenta-
    tion at the Strategic Management Society, Boston, October 1987.
"Leaders who can't execute . . .": Larry Bossidy and Ram Charan, *Execution,*
    p. 5.
"Execution is a discipline . . .": Larry Bossidy and Ram Charan, *Execution,* p. 21.
"Having an execution discipline . . .": "Execution as Attitude," *The Chief
    Executive,* May 2002.
Develop an "architecture for execution": Larry Bossidy and Ram Charan,
    Execution, p. 28.
"Change can't occur without laser-like accountability . . .": "Execution as
    Attitude," *The Chief Executive,* May 2002.
"If you don't measure it, it doesn't get done": "Execution as Attitude," *The Chief
    Executive,* May 2002.
"Six Sigma has been successful at Honeywell . . .": "Execution as Attitude," *The
    Chief Executive,* May 2002.
Bossidy's passion concerning Six Sigma is covered in Smith et al., *Strategic Six
    Sigma* (New York: Wiley, Sept. 13, 2002).
"Confirming and institutionalizing or sustaining process improvements . . .":
    "Execution as Attitude," *The Chief Executive,* May 2002.

Chapter 8

"Our core purpose is to improve . . .": Ibid.
Welch's description of Nardelli's financial performance comes from Jack
    Welch, *Jack: Straight from the Gut,* p. 427.
"Jack and I used to marvel . . .": Patricia Sellers, "Something to Prove," *Fortune*
    June 24, 2002, p. 7.
"I added a couple of E's . . .": Interview with Robert Nardelli, Feb. 3, 2005.
"I was afforded a tremendous amount...": Ibid.
"What I learned was the ability . . .": Ibid.
"Putting these three stars into these new jobs . . .": Jack Welch, *Jack: Straight from
    the Gut,* p. 416.
"You probably could not feel worse . . .": Patricia Sellers, "Something to Prove,"
    Fortune, June 24, 2002, p. 7.
The discussion of Home Depot's hiring of Nardelli comes from Patricia Sellers,
    "Something to Prove," *Fortune,* June 24, 2002, p. 7.

The discussion of Home Depot's problems comes from Thottam and Fulton, "Bob the Builder," *Time Canada,* June 21, 2004.

"Under Jack Welch, GE developed the deepest bench . . .": Diane Brady, *Business Week,* Oct. 25, 2004, p. 20.

We weren't in the home supply business . . .": Interview with Robert Nardelli, Feb. 3, 2005.

The discussion regarding Home Depot's $600 million expenditure on training comes from interview with Robert Nardelli, Feb. 3, 2005

". . .The ability to connect the dots. . . .": Interview with Robert Nardelli, Feb. 3, 2005.

The discussion of Home Depot's problems comes from Thottam and Fulton, "Bob the Builder," *Time Canada,* June 21, 2004.

"It was like having nine different wives": Dan Morse, "A Hardware Chain Struggles to Adjust to a New Blueprint," *Wall Street Journal,* Jan. 17, 2003, p. A1, A6.

The description of the company's drowning in paper comes from *Business Week,* Oct. 25, 2004.

". . .We have tried to create here . . .": Interview with Robert Nardelli, Feb. 3, 2005.

"It is a company that has grown up with its cofounders. . . .": Carol Hymowitz, Interview with Robert Nardelli, Stern Chief Executive Series, Fall/Winter 2003.

". . .We now communicate regularly . . .": Interview with Robert Nardelli, Feb. 3, 2005.

". . .We'll talk about succession planning . . .": Ibid.

"Our strategy was very simple. . . .": Ron Insana, "Fixer-Uppers Spruce Up Profit at Home Depot," USA Today.com, July 6, 2004; and Bob Nardelli, *Home Depot Annual Report,* March 29, 2004.

"Under each of those three. . . .": Interview with Robert Nardelli, Feb. 3, 2005.

The discussion regarding "SOAR" and Home Depot's performance matrix, ibid.

"I think you have to identify your strategy . . .": Carol Hymowitz, Interview with Robert Nardelli, Stern Chief Executive Series, Fall/Winter 2003.

"I learned from experience. . . .": Patricia Sellers, "Something to Prove," *Fortune,* June 24, 2002, p. 7.

"I wish I had moved faster . . .": Patricia Sellers and Julie Schlosser, *Fortune* interview, Sept. 20, 2004.

The criticism of GE's divesting the housewares division is quoted in Noel Tichy and Stratford Sherman, *Control Your Own Destiny or Someone Else Will,* p. 87.

"The rate of internal change . . .": Patricia Sellers, "Something to Prove," *Fortune* June 24, 2002, p. 7.

"Through our service business, we are positioned . . .": Bob Nardelli, Home Depot Annual Report, March 29, 2004.

Nardelli's reining in of Home Depot comes from Dan Morse, "Under Renovation," *Wall Street Journal.*

"I love the entrepreneurial spirit. . . .": Dan Morse, "Under Renovation," *Wall Street Journal.*

"What we're looking for is . . .": Carol Hymowitz, Interview with Robert Nardelli, Stern Chief Executive Series, Fall/Winter 2003.

"We have a real passion . . .": Carol Hymowitz, Interview with Robert Nardelli, Stern Chief Executive Series, Fall/Winter 2003.

Chapter 9

"This is only a transition . . .": Bharat Kumar, "Business Line's Investment World, The Hindu Group,"May 6, 2001.

"Do we want to be number one?": Vivek Paul, quoted in Ashai Rai, "Paul Work and No Play," *Economic Times,* Aug. 10, 2002.

"In the 1990s we learned . . .": Vivek Paul, Eric Lundquist interview, *eWeek,* Feb. 23, 2004.

Drucker's reference to CEO "geniuses or supermen" comes from Peter Drucker, *Concept of the Corporations,* 1946, p. 26.

"You can build another skyscraper . . .": Jyoti Thottam, "Wipro Technologies," *Time,* Dec. 12, 2004.

The problem with the psyches of Wipro employees and Paul's determination to come up with a plan to deal with it is discussed in Mitu Jayashankar, "The Comeback," *Businessworld,* Feb. 9, 2004.

"Go after initiative . . .": Ashai Rai, "Paul Work and No Play," *Economic Times,* Aug. 10, 2002.

"Knowledge is the business . . .": Peter Drucker, *Managing for Results* (New York: Harper Collins, 1967), p. 111.

Paul's description of Wipro as a "global back-office for hire" comes from "An American in Bangalore," *Economist,* Feb. 6, 2003.

"We don't try to architect the perfect solution . . .": Ashai Rai, "Paul Work and No Play," *Economic Times,* Aug. 10, 2002.

"I think you have to consider the slowdown in context. . . .": Bharat Kumar, "Business Line's Investment World, The Hindu Group," May 6, 2001.

"There is much opportunity out there. . . .": Bharat Kumar, "Business Line's Investment World, The Hindu Group," May 6, 2001.

"For 30 percent less than that . . .": "Tech Guru Loves Wipro's Vivek Paul," *Economic Times,* Feb. 18, 2004.

"We are moving to a world . . .": Vivek Paul, Eric Lundquist interview, *eWeek,* Feb. 23, 2004.

Paul's learning about the importance of values at GE is discussed in Ashai Rai, "Paul Work and No Play," *Economic Times,* Aug. 10, 2002.

"You go down a path . . .": Ashai Rai, "Paul Work and No Play," *Economic Times,* Aug. 10, 2002.

"From the first day in dealing with Wipro . . .": Wipro Technology Web site.

"We answered the question . . .": Vivek Paul, Eric Lundquist interview, *eWeek,* Feb. 23, 2004.

"What has happened . . . over the last few years . . .": Vivek Paul, Eric Lundquist interview, *eWeek,* Feb. 23, 2004.

"I think of ourselves as a global company . . .": Vivek Paul, Eric Lundquist interview, *eWeek,* Feb. 23, 2004.

Backmatter

"And yet the ultimate test of management . . .": Peter Drucker, *The Practice of Management,* pp. 9–10.

INDEX

ABOUT THE AUTHOR

Jeffrey A. Krames is the bestselling author of *The Welch Way*, *The Jack Welch Lexicon of Leadership*, and *What the Best CEOs Know*, two of which have been named Best Leadership Books of the Year by Library Journal. A frequent guest on CNN, CNBC, and Fox News Channel, Krames has written for the *New York Times*, the *Wall Street Journal*, and the *Los Angeles Times*.